NEVER,
EVER GIVE
UP?

NEVER, EVER GIVE UP?

A memoir

John Hellemans

CANTERBURY UNIVERSITY PRESS

First published in 2018 by
CANTERBURY UNIVERSITY PRESS
University of Canterbury
Private Bag 4800, Christchurch
NEW ZEALAND
www.canterbury.ac.nz/engage/cup

ISBN 978-1-98-850305-9

A catalogue record for this book is available from the
National Library of New Zealand.

Book design and layout: Smartwork Creative, www.smartworkcreative.co.nz

Front cover image: World age-group championships, Queenstown, 2003.
© Endurance Sport

Printed by Caxton, New Zealand

For Ocean, Lakey, Johanna, Harrison and Nico

I do not know the truth; only my memories.
– From *Augustus* by John Williams

Contents

Foreword

Luck, coincidence, timing ... do they find you, or do you find them? I'm not quite sure how I came to be coached by John, but it was probably a mix of all three.

There he was, an undisclosed sports addict, and there was me – a young woman searching for something to excel at. I'm not sure either of us knew how new triathlon was. We had read about it, and both of us were inspired by the Les Mills Triathlon in Auckland, but we didn't know the sport was in its infancy.

No matter – he became my coach, and I trusted him instantly and implicitly. John had the academic ability, the fire of a young man fighting some of his upbringing and great intuition on training. Back then, there were no heart-rate monitors, power meters or flash bikes with aerobars – just training.

I guess his early approach could have failed. But with two very capable athletes, him and me, it didn't. He gave me workouts, I did them. There was only one session I didn't complete. He found out later that day, and told me to get out and do it – freezing rain or not.

He says he experimented on me with training sessions, but the whole thing was one big experiment, and I was just lucky he was a person with tremendous intuition. He had a very willing and able pupil, but I knew I was pushing my 'master', when, instead of joining in the session, he would break out the stopwatch and want to observe.

After reading John's book, I felt embarrassed that I never really knew him. I was just very good at the sport, but he embraced it, in the same way my husband, Scott Molina, does. I truly never got that, but when I read this book, his passion became abundantly clear.

In so many small ways, John only just missed the boat in becoming a professional triathlete himself. He had the entire skill set. However, he was already married with a young family, was a doctor, and he had a keen sense of his responsibility to family and occupation.

John has written an account that had me alternately laughing and crying as I read it. It's not just a book for triathletes, but for anyone who wants to read about a journey through life, as he also tells us about his parents and his adventures as a young doctor in his adopted country of New Zealand. It's a fabulous read. I have learned a great deal not only about the sport, but about my former coach. It's been a humbling experience.

It has also given me insight into the other wonderful athletes John has coached. His passion for the sport has been felt around the planet with the many athletes he has successfully mentored. His 'firm Dutch ways' have mellowed over the years, as he has learned to deal with the many personality types he has worked with. Readers will see he has assisted the lives of many people.

This book provides a fascinating introduction to the sport of triathlon – its personalities and its progression to the Olympic sport it is today. John has been there from the beginning, and still is to this day. He's a great husband, father, grandfather, doctor, friend, coach – and, now, author.

Erin Baker MBE
Christchurch, 2018

Preface

The new sport of triathlon reached the shores of New Zealand in 1979, when the first event was held along the Auckland waterfront. By chance I saw an item about the race on a television news bulletin. A new immigrant from the Netherlands, I had been in New Zealand for less than a year.

I was intrigued by the footage of the Auckland triathlon. With a background in competitive swimming, a newly discovered talent for running, and the knowledge that every Dutchman can ride a bike, I decided I could do that. It wasn't until 1982 that I got to Auckland to compete in that event. It was the start of a long career in the sport, as a coach and administrator and as a competitor.

I combined my triathlon activities with a career in general practice and sports medicine. Early on I became known for my success as a competitor, but later achieved a reputation more as coach and advisor for some of New Zealand's best-performing triathletes. Of these Erin Baker was the first and the best. She became one of the most successful woman triathletes the sport has seen, and the highlights of her career are recounted in the first chapter. Erin and I were at the forefront of this new sport, which swept the world in the 1980s and 90s. One of my motives in writing this book was to tell some of Erin's story; I hope to provide an insight into her unique personality and show why she should be remembered for more than her 10 world championship titles.

My association with Erin resulted in other athletes approaching me for assistance. I set to work and became a proper coach. Among the athletes whose stories are told here, Kris Gemmell and Andrea Hewitt get special attention. Details of their preparation for the Beijing Olympic Games give the reader a rare behind-the-scenes perspective on the brutal world of Olympic qualification, preparation and competition.

A few months before the 2011 Christchurch earthquake, I was appointed head coach for the Dutch triathlon team. Returning to my country of birth was a bitter-sweet experience of nostalgic familiarity, mixed with frustration and at times despair.

The Hawaii Ironman is still considered the holy grail of the triathlon sport by purists and I try to answer the question of what motivates us to expose ourselves to the suffering we experience when we engage in such extreme endurance events. I resisted the temptation to compete in the Hawaii Ironman for a long time, until I was 60 – old enough to know better – when I finally succumbed to the challenge to prove myself a 'real triathlete'. It nearly proved to be a bridge too far.

This book is not only about the history of triathlon in New Zealand as experienced by a coach and athlete, but also about growing up in Europe under the threat of the Cold War, and life as an immigrant in a new country, having to adjust to a different culture and its customs.

It wasn't until I was confronted with New Zealand's sporting culture of pride, passion and perseverance that I understood that perseverance is one of the most important attributes for success in sport and probably in life. There is a saying we often hear in sport: 'no failure, just feedback'. Of course there is failure and there are times when it's right to pull back, or even give up and re-group. I don't know of any successful person that hasn't had one or more experiences like that. But if it's reframed as an opportunity to gain more knowledge, strengthen resolve and be better prepared next time, it helps us to develop the necessary resilience and move on.

For the last few years writing has become my part-time obsession. Short periods of frenzied writing were interrupted for months at a time when life, as they say, got in the way. I have had to rehash and rewrite, and consign a lot of it to the wastepaper basket, but in persisting I've discovered that I enjoy writing about my experiences as much as, if not more than, the experiences themselves.

CHAPTER 1
ERIN BAKER

European Ironman Championships, Almere, 1985

It's 17 August 1985, the day of Erin Baker's international ironman race debut at the inaugural European Ironman Championships in the Netherlands – and it does not start well.

Despite it being mid-summer, the weather is atrocious, with thunder, lightning and horizontal rain, which has free reign over the barren landscape. The race is being held at Almere, which is Holland's youngest city, built on land reclaimed in the 1960s. There is little in the way of natural shelter on the flat land just outside the city. The weather forces a delayed start, and the swim distance is cut from the customary 3.8km to 2.4km. The Ijsselmeer – a large, closed-off inlet – resembles a tumultuous sea.

Erin is in a bad mood because of all this, but also because of the Dutch officials' anal approach at the early morning check-in. The Dutch are sticklers for rules. Erin, a free-spirited Kiwi, doesn't cope well with the demands placed on her this morning regarding compulsory use of gear bags, numbering, bike placement and limited access to certain areas. I have lived in New Zealand for six years by now and understand her frustration. Add pre-race nerves and she's so wound up she is ready to strangle one of the officials … and she nearly does.

I find an unlocked car near the transition area and instruct Erin to take shelter inside it and have some time for herself. I stand guard outside. A large man identified as an 'OFFICIAL' by his yellow vest, his face partly hidden by a sizeable beard, comes storming towards me. He growls in Dutch, wondering what she is doing in his car. Before I can stop him, he opens the door and tells Erin to get out. Although Erin doesn't understand Dutch, she gets the gist.

Already on edge, she explodes. She closes her hands around the man's neck and screams at him to leave her alone. His eyes nearly pop out of their sockets and his face quickly turns dark blue. I step in and rescue him in the nick of time. I suggest that he makes himself scarce, as if it is all his fault. To my surprise he does, scuttling away like a scared rabbit.

Erin takes control of the race on the bike, gradually pulling away from her main rivals, who include Sarah Springman from England, the American Ardis Bow and German champion Gabriela Hirsemann.

At the last minute, I had given Erin my black waterproof jacket to put on after the swim, to protect her from the cold and rain. With the black cloak flapping in the wind, she looks like a furious Dracula on a bike (minus the fangs), but it doesn't slow her down and when she comes past at the 100km mark of the 180km bike section, she has built a healthy 20-minute lead over her pursuers. I relax and seek shelter from the arctic conditions in a café, as it will be a while before she comes past again.

The race is beamed live on national television. I settle down with a mug of hot soup and a view of the big screen. The camera is focused on an intriguing battle between the two leading men, Gregor Stam and Rob Barel. I am slowly pulled in by their cat and mouse game.

Officials on motorbikes repeatedly warn them with loud whistles when they threaten to get too close to each other. The Dutch have always been strong advocates of the non-drafting rule and are strict on its implementation.[1] The two riders play the game well, trying to get protection from the surrounding motorbikes when they can't get it from each other.

Suddenly, the camera switches to a commotion on the side of the road. The commentator tries to work out what is going on. A competitor has a puncture, he informs us. I'm dismayed they have to show this just as the action at the front of the field is heating up.

Then I jolt upright. The competitor standing on the side of the road, wrestling to remove the deflated tyre from her wheel, is Erin Baker. The commentator recognises Erin at the same time I do and gets excited. He notices she doesn't seem to have the strength to pull the tyre off the rim. He wonders what this athlete, who has travelled all the way from the other side of the world, is going to do next.

Initially, I'm not worried. Erin knows how to change a tyre. After all, she has had enough practice. During her training rides, she always insisted on fixing any 'flatty' herself, steadfastly declining help offered by her training partners on the basis that one day she might need the skills during a race.

But Erin is not prepared for changing a tyre in freezing weather. Despite the jacket, she is so cold and wet she has lost all feeling in her hands. The tubular tyre is glued on tight and does not come off. A bystander, feeling sorry for her, steps forward, offering his help. He tries to take the wheel off her. Erin is well aware that receiving help will result in instant disqualification, so she doesn't let go of the wheel. With increasing anxiety, I watch the tug of war with the bike wheel unfold on the big screen. A Dutch official on a motorbike is standing close to Erin, glaring suspiciously at her actions. Erin decides to take the initiative, grabs her bike pump with her free hand, and whacks the Good Samaritan firmly around his ears, telling him in no uncertain terms – in a voice clearly audible to all the viewers – to back off.

More than 20 minutes have gone by and the first of the pursuing female competitors comes past. Erin gets back to work with renewed vigour, but the tyre doesn't budge. Another competitor comes past and then another. I bury my face in my hands, unable to watch any longer.

At this stage, if not before, most of us would have called it a day, collected our appearance money and gone home for a warm bath, secretly pleased to have a valid excuse to escape potential defeat, the foul weather and the miseries that can be expected with the marathon run, still to come.

Not Erin.

The pub patrons have gradually been drawn in by the live drama playing out on the screen. A loud cheer goes up and I lift my head to see Erin ripping the tyre off the wheel with her teeth. My neighbour looks at me with eyes like saucers and asks which planet this woman is from. 'Aotearoa,' I blurt out. Before the man can ask where the bloody hell in the universe that is, I jump up and leave. I have to get back on the course to give Erin her splits and a hurry-up.

By the time she starts the marathon run, Erin is back in the lead. She goes on to win the women's race from Sarah Springman by nearly an hour, and she places 7th overall.

Like mother, like daughter

The tenacity and bloody-mindedness displayed by Erin Baker in winning the European Ironman Championships in Holland in 1985 became the hallmark of her career. In part, her attitude and personality can be explained by her background. She is the fifth-born in a family of eight, and, to support the family, her father, freezing worker Brian Baker, supplemented his income with one or sometimes two additional jobs.

Erin's mother, Mary, gave up paid work to become an activist for peace and justice: 'There will be no peace without justice' was and still is her favourite quote. Her focus became the anti-Apartheid movement, an international drive that flourished in the 1970s and 80s in opposition to South Africa's system of racial oppression. Mary was an active member of Halt All Racist Tours (HART). They opposed apartheid by focusing on something many New Zealanders cared about deeply – sport, in particular rugby. Their main target was South Africa's national team, the Springboks, the nemesis of New Zealanders' beloved All Blacks; the Springboks had no black players in their team, despite the fact that blacks outnumbered whites in South Africa by eight to one.

It all came to a head during the 1981 tour of New Zealand when in fact the South Africans did have one black player, Errol Tobias, on their team; his inclusion was criticised as a token gesture. By a quirk of fate, Mary, who was returning from a visit to relatives in America, found herself travelling on the same plane as the Springboks, who were on their way to start their tour in New Zealand. She didn't waste the opportunity for direct confrontation, telling them they weren't wanted and asking Errol Tobias why he was selling out. Somehow she managed to avoid being offloaded en route via Hawaii, and towards the end of the flight she launched a one-woman demonstration in front of a captive audience, writing 'SHAME' on a sick-bag in red biro, which she marched up and down the plane while her fellow passengers were locked in by their breakfast trays. Mary recalls that the Springboks were dumbfounded by her protest, too stunned to respond, but she got abuse from other New Zealanders.

As soon as the Springboks arrived in New Zealand numerous protest marches took place all over the country. Protesters didn't limit themselves to the streets, but also invaded rugby pitches before and during games, resulting in physical confrontations with diehard rugby fans. The country was divided, tempers flared, not only on the street but also in communities and even within families.

Mary chaired the Christchurch Coalition Against the Tour. Armed with a megaphone, she was in the frontline of the protests, with Erin never far from her side. Then one day Erin threw a smoke bomb at police trying to control a demonstration and she was arrested, along with many others. Some were charged with disorderly behavior, but most were let off. However, once the authorities found out that Erin was the daughter of Mary Baker, she was charged with the much more serious offence of 'possessing and throwing of an incendiary device with intent to injure'. Erin was found guilty and ordered to serve 200 hours of community service. She lost her job as a radiographer at Christchurch Hospital and, disillusioned, moved to Darwin in Australia to start her life afresh. There, she discovered the new sport of triathlon. Her parents had always encouraged their kids to play sports and Erin had been a competitive swimmer and runner. She soon found she was also a natural on the bike.

Getting started

In 1983, still in Australia, Erin entered her first triathlon. She called me for some last-minute tips before that race. We had never met but were members of the same running club in Christchurch and she'd heard about my triathlon exploits.

During that first race, Erin's seat post broke when she jumped on her bike after the swim, most likely due to a faulty seat bolt. She was forced to do the bike leg in standing position, but she still won. To this day, she maintains her bike was sabotaged.

When Erin called me after the race to report back, she suggested I come to Australia for the Queensland Triathlon Championships to be held in Mooloolaba a few weeks later. She added that all the top Aussies would be there and a few of the American pros.

I bumped into her just before the start of the race. The first thing that struck me was that she did not look like an athlete: she was small in stature, with a stocky build. However, her features – her penetrating brown eyes and tightly pursed lips (topped off with her cap of fiery red hair) – displayed the determination she became known for.

Erin won the women's race and I won the men's. For a Kiwi, beating the Australians on their home soil is almost like winning a gold medal at the Olympics. We became instant mates.

Erin had a clear vision of where the sport was heading. Confidently she told me triathlon was the sport of the future. One day there would be official world championships and it could even become an Olympic sport. I just laughed. Triathlon was still unregulated, with several types of events run over different distances and using different disciplines. There was no structure, no standards, no organisation, not even a representative body.

>>>

Erin returned to Christchurch to train full-time. We discussed ideas about training, some we made up, some were taken from other sports. I had become an avid believer in the training methods of New Zealand running coach Arthur Lydiard. I went training with Erin when I could, but often I did not have time between work and family. I would suggest a certain training session to her. When she liked the session, I put it into my own training programme; when she came home half-dead, I knew to avoid it. She became my guinea pig. She had time to experiment, I didn't, and she didn't seem to mind this arrangement. It got her fit, and she beat her opposition by increasing margins. While Mark Allen, Scott Tinley, Scott Molina and Dave Scott were setting the standards in North America in training and racing, edging each other along, Erin did the same for the women, singlehandedly, based out of 'little old New Zealand'.

One of those training sessions that has survived the test of time is the Mount Pleasant Hill repetitions. On the outskirts of Christchurch, Mount Pleasant forms part of the Port Hills. The road to the top is 4.5km long, with an average gradient of 8%. Just over halfway, there is a large water tank hidden from the road. I suggested Erin bike up to the water tank, then dismount and change into her running shoes for a dash to the summit. The bike section took her 11–15 minutes and the run 7 to 10 minutes, depending on her effort.

Two to three repetitions, sometimes four, done at different intensities, turned out to be an effective strength-endurance session. It's physically tough, and a good mental work out, too. It is still used today by local and visiting international athletes, who, some time ago, renamed the hill 'Mount Unpleasant'.

>>>

America was leading the way in triathlon in the 1980s, with lots of media interest, many races to choose from, prize money and sponsorships. It made sense for Erin to go there and try her luck – except for one minor snag: her conviction meant a visa for the US was out of the question. A frustrating three years of applying, being turned down and re-applying followed. When, in 1984, Prime Minister David Lange declared New Zealand nuclear free and barred nuclear-powered or armed ships from entering our ports, the American administration was less inclined to do New Zealanders any favours. Erin's visa application became a victim of the stand-off between our little country and its big cousin.

Meanwhile, Erin made a name for herself competing in Australia and Europe. The second biggest race on the international triathlon calendar after the Hawaii Ironman was the French Nice triathlon, known as the World Long Distance Triathlon Championships. The race had more manageable distances, with a 4km swim, a 120km bike leg and a 32km run. It became Erin's favourite event, which she won four times, the first in 1986.

The cycling-mad French public embraced the event, which had a bike course of epic proportions, resembling a mountain stage of the Tour de France. It was one of the few races the Americans bothered to travel to Europe for. The French love their sport almost as much as their wine, and for many years the Nice event rivalled the Hawaii Ironman in popularity. Erin's dominance in the event earned her a lucrative sponsorship deal with French clothing company Le Coq Sportif.

She didn't have it all her way in Nice. One year she was disqualified under the ruling 'no outside assistance allowed' when she took a drink from her sister, who was a spectator at the run.

It was not uncommon for other participants to do the same, because the organisers were never generous with the placement of drink stations, despite the hot conditions. Erin had the misfortune to be caught on camera and someone put in a protest. The story goes that CBS owned the rights for the event and it suited them to have American winners. For the men, that was no problem; Mark Allen won the event 10 times. But Erin had spoiled the party once too often.

At the next race, a year later, I received a phone call at midnight from Erin to let me know that she had won the race and there had been no trouble. 'Very nice, well done,' I said and tried to go back to sleep. The phone woke me again at 4am. Erin told me that after four hours at the drug-testing facility she still did not have the urge to go to the toilet. It was obvious that during the race she had not drunk enough, petrified to take fluids from the public outside the designated drink stations. She was dehydrated and now she had difficulty producing the requested urine sample.

The French doctor was getting suspicious, wondering if she was trying to avoid the testing. He had announced he wanted to do a bladder puncture, so Erin thought she better call me to get my opinion. I couldn't believe it and asked if she was sure. Maybe the doctor's English wasn't very good, and Erin's French was certainly non-existent, so there was potential for misunderstanding.

But Erin was adamant they wanted to stick a great big needle through her abdominal wall into her bladder to suck out any potential evidence. I told her to refuse, request a lawyer, drink heaps and play for time, because it was inevitable that soon she would be able to come up with the goods. She did refuse, and to the relief of all involved she managed to oblige a short time later.

I got another call from her to confirm that, just when I was once more drifting back to sleep.

The French prize money was good and her sponsorship deal with Le Coq Sportif paid her more than the Americans ever would. But Erin was still desperate to get to the land of milk and honey, where the competition was – and the Hawaii Ironman, which at the time was considered the ultimate triathlon event. In the end, it required intervention from Minister of Foreign Affairs Russell Marshall to plead on Erin's behalf directly with the American authorities. In June 1986, she was finally granted her US visa. However, her first attempt at the Hawaii Ironman that same year was an anti-climax. She had been ill in the weeks before the race but ignored the warning signs. When she found herself well back in the field, she admitted defeat and withdrew.

The Hawaii Ironman World Championships

Since the inclusion of triathlon in the Olympic Games in 2000, the shorter Olympic-distance version has become the flagship for the sport, but for purists the Ironman World Championships held in Hawaii every year in early October remain the holy grail.

In 1978, US naval officer John Collins set a challenge to combine the Waikiki Rough Water Swim (3.8km), the Around Oahu Bike Race (180km) and the Honolulu Marathon (42km) to decide which athletes were the fittest swimmers, cyclists and runners. 'The winner can call himself an ironman,' he announced. The pre-race handout, totalling three pages of rules and course description, ended with the handwritten note: 'Swim 2.4 miles! Bike 112 miles! Run 26.2 miles! Brag for the rest of your life!'

Three weeks following the challenge set by John Collins, on 18 February, 15 athletes started the race and 12 finished. Gordon Haller, a US Navy communication specialist, finished in 11 hours, 46 minutes and 58 seconds to become the first-ever Ironman. Runner-up, US Navy Seal John Dunbar, led the race for a long time but ran out of water during the run and resorted to drinking beer, which was not conducive to running in a straight line. Haller passed him around the 35km mark.

Thereafter the race was held on a yearly basis and quickly gained popularity. In 1981, it was moved to Kailua-Kona on the much quieter 'Big Island' – Hawaii Island – which has been its home ever since.

The Hawaii Ironman is considered one of the top 10 toughest sporting events in the world. The media is fascinated by the feast of suffering dished up against a background of black lava fields and brutal climatic conditions. Simmering heat rises visibly from the black, tar-sealed roads, enveloping a long line of suffering, emaciated bodies, hardened by months of relentless training. Faces initially confident and determined turn gaunt and expressionless. The body and mind scream 'no more', yet, somehow, something makes the athletes persevere.

It is a Mecca for reality TV, as nothing fascinates more than the pain, agonies and struggles of other people. Julie Moss's televised dramatic crawl across the finish line in 1982, soiled pants and all, catapulted ironman triathlon from obscurity to worldwide fame. Paula Newby-Fraser hitting the wall in 1995, dropping from 1st to 4th, is one of the most watched ironman video clips of all time. It was described by English commentator and journalist Phil Liggett as one of the most memorable moments of ABC television coverage. Two years later, a different commentator witnessed the desperate collapse and subsequent crawling race towards the finish line by Wendy Ingraham and Sian Welch. 'The body obliterated, but the spirit held firm,' he intoned. They were fighting it out for 4th place.

The big question is: what drives people to do this to themselves? Books have been written and endless documentaries made in search of an answer. 'Out of suffering have emerged the strongest souls; the most massive characters are seared with scars,' wrote Khalil Gibran, and the Nietzschean maxim that what does not kill us makes us stronger is often quoted to help us get through adversity. That isn't always true, of course. Post-traumatic stress following wars, accidents and natural disasters is all too common. In contrast to wars and disasters, the participation in extreme endurance events is voluntary. By taking part, we actively seek out the suffering and hardship, not only during the event but also in the lead-up, in order to condition ourselves for what is to come.

The dedication and application required to train for and finish an ironman can turn into an obsession resulting in a loss of perspective and dire consequences. So, why do we risk injury, illness, relationships and a disabling fatigue, the magnitude of which is normally reserved for the terminally ill? Are the challenges thrown at us during our normal daily lives not enough? Is it that we want to prove we can do something extraordinary? Do we seek some sort of approval or confirmation? Why is it that my finisher medals from the few ultra-endurance events I've done mean as much as, if not more than, my national and international victories over the shorter distances?

Perhaps it's because extreme sporting events strip you of the niceties and pretence that take over when all is going well, and expose the naked truth of who we really are. In *The End of History and the Last Man* Francis Fukuyama suggests that we are drawn to activities involving competitive achievements and personal challenges to avoid staring into the abyss of pointlessness that is opened up by modern living in a liberal democracy. Fukuyama wonders whether merely making money or getting elected to political office are hollow victories; perhaps transcendent challenges are ultimately necessary. It is the antidote for the observers of life we have become, rather than being participants. 'Because it's there,' George Mallory answered when asked why he wanted to climb Mount Everest. He paid the ultimate price and never returned.

The bigger the challenge, the finer the line between being a hero and a nobody, a loser, or even dead. But this is rarely mentioned in the documentaries and books. It is almost always about willpower and overcoming the odds and hardship, giving it a false sense of romance that in its turn spurs others on to pursue similar goals.

Hawaii Ironman, 1987

For Erin Baker, there was nothing romantic about doing the ironman. For her, it was simply a question of business. She knew that to survive financially she had to do ironman events. To make a decent living, as a non-American, she not only had to race in the Ironman World Championship event in Hawaii, but, more importantly, win it. It was as simple as that.

If she had been born 20 years later she would have been happy to make a living from the shorter distance World Cup and World Series races and avoid the ironman altogether. Erin recognised the madness of the ironman event, but at the same time was unable to avoid it. This dilemma became the source of a love-hate relationship she developed with the sport during her career.

After her failed appearance in 1986, the next year Erin invited my wife, Ien, and me to travel to Hawaii to support her in her second attempt. This time she was determined to get it right. Her preparation back home in New Zealand was meticulous. Thirty-hour training weeks were unheard-of at the time. Those, combined with a carefully thought-out race strategy and nutrition plan, were going to give her a fighting chance for a podium finish. On paper she was the best, but reputations mean nothing in Hawaii and we had to wait and see how Erin – fair-skinned and used to a more temperate climate – would cope with the searing conditions.

A few weeks before the 1987 Hawaii Ironman, Erin finished 6th at the International Bermuda Triathlon, a big-money race that attracted a strong international field. The race is remembered mainly for the fact that a young 15-year-old upstart from America by the name of Lance Armstrong finished third in a stacked field, not far behind superstars Mike Allen and Mike Pigg. Seven athletes, including big names like Scott Molina, Dave Scott and Glenn Cook, were disqualified for blatant drafting. Scott Molina later admitted it had been the only way to keep the unleashed youngster in sight.

Her 6th was Erin's worst-ever result. She did the race to earn some much-needed cash to assist her ironman preparations. Granted, we didn't adjust her ironman training and fitted the event in as a training race, but we still expected at least a top-three finish, if not a customary win.

When I asked her what had happened she explained she was toasted from the heat and sun by the time she hit the run. She also said that all the top-ranked women were racing with crazy-looking new handlebars. The day before the race, Erin was puzzled when Joy Hansen, in her drawling American accent, had asked her if she had the new bras. Erin soon forgot the weird question, until Joy came storming past on the bike, body in horizontal position – and Erin realised she had not said 'bras', but 'bars'. She had been able to keep up with the other competitors going uphill, but on the downhill and flat sections of the course they would lie down on their new handlebars and ride away from her.

We learned some valuable lessons from the Bermuda race. First, Erin needed to get hold of this new handlebar invention to even the playing field. The 'aerobars', now a mainstream item on any triathlete's bike, allow the rider to rest their elbows on the handlebars with the forearms stretched in front, resulting in a superior aerodynamic body position. We had some sent over from America, and tests quickly confirmed the new bars would give Erin an estimated time gain of 10 minutes over the 180km ironman bike distance.

The aerobar suited our sport perfectly, because every race was a time trial where aerodynamics counts for much. Of course, I had to have them too, but they were very expensive and I decided they could easily be made locally. One of my patients, who was an aircraft engineer for Air New Zealand, made a couple of straight bars that could be clamped onto my handlebars. He was worried about potential breakage (presumably something always front-of-mind for any self-respecting aircraft engineer), so he made them strong. Consequently, they weighed a ton. I cut up some pull buoys (the type used between the legs to provide buoyancy when swimming with arms only) and fixed them around the top of my handlebars. Using them to rest my forearms on, I was ready to surprise the opposition. When I turned up at the next race in Auckland, my smugness didn't last long when I discovered the other athletes hadn't sat still either. They turned up with similar contraptions, negating any potential advantage.

The difficulties Erin experienced in Bermuda with the heat were harder to overcome. In Christchurch's August and September winter–spring months, temperatures rarely exceed single digits. Erin put on extra layers of clothing when biking and running, but their additional effect on the production of body heat did not come even close to mimicking the harsh conditions she was going to face in Hawaii. We decided to go across to Hawaii a few days earlier than planned, to acclimatise to the extreme conditions.

In 1987 Erin's main opposition was the winner from the previous year, ironman specialist Paula Newby-Fraser, racing for Zimbabwe. The Puntous twins from Canada, Sylviane and Patricia, lined up for the start as well. Sylviane had won the race in 1983 and 1984, with Patricia coming 2nd on both occasions.

Erin not only had Paula to contend with, but also Paula's protection squad, consisting of her partner Paul Huddle, her friend Mark Montgomery and their cronies. They were known to form a protective shield around her during the swim and the early part of the bike leg. This irked Erin greatly, but it was within the rules. She could have done the same, but she felt it was not in the spirit of the race. We also figured that between us we didn't have enough friends to make it work.

There were three main components to Erin's race strategy. The first was her trademark tactic of taking the lead on the bike early on and not relinquishing it. She was never the fastest swimmer, but was close enough for this simple plan to be effective, because she was so strong on the bike. The second part concerned her nutrition. We knew that in ironman events nutrition is the fourth discipline and Ien, who is a sports dietitian, had designed a detailed nutrition and hydration plan for Erin to follow on the day.

The third and final strategy was never going to be guessed by her opposition until it was too late. Historically, on the odd occasion Erin did not come off the bike in first position, she could always make it up on the run. But I was not convinced about this for Hawaii. I felt that under the extreme conditions, the other more experienced women could potentially match Erin on the run over that distance. I had noticed when we viewed coverage from previous races that everyone walked through the aid stations, which were positioned exactly one mile apart along the marathon route on the out and back course. 'Recover and re-energise at the aid stations,' was the word, and all competitors did. Everybody walked as if their lives depended on it. But it didn't make sense to me. When you keep changing between running and walking, you not only lose considerable time, but also your rhythm.

I convinced Erin to keep running through the aid stations, but not to forego the drinks. We worked out a technique whereby on the run she could pour water from a cup down her throat without choking. It was done by squeezing the cup while throwing it back and timing her swallow with the rhythm of her step. I calculated she would gain at least five seconds per aid station. Over the 25 stations that was a two-minute gain for little extra energy expenditure.

Erin had a rough swim. Age groupers and pros all started together and then it was a shit-fight – as it is now – in which she drew the short straw. She came out of the water battered and bruised, a few minutes down on the leaders, who included Paula, usually a slower swimmer than Erin. It took Erin until the bike turnaround to catch her.

I managed to position myself at the base of a hill with 40km of the bike still to go. First the men came past, led by Mark Allen with Dave Scott not far behind. Their pursuers were already far back and well spread out. The wait for Erin in the hot, shadeless conditions out on the lava fields was unbearable. Would she be leading? Where the bloody hell was she? The lights of the lead motorbike became visible from a distance. The notorious headwinds at that part of the course had forced Erin's pace down to a crawl. She didn't look happy when she came past, but then I had never known her to be in a good mood during race time. Within minutes Sylviane and

Paula came past, riding close together. I was worried. Erin hit the run in front, but by only a couple of minutes.

Before the race, Erin had asked me to leave a hat on the road for her, 3km into the run. It would give her the option to pick it up before she got onto the Queen K Highway if the sun was out on the unprotected lava fields. The rules prohibited me from handing it to her. What we had not counted on was the thick row of spectators. They looked at me strangely when I wrestled to the front row to deposit the hat on the road as I saw her approaching.

Everyone roared loudly when they saw Erin coming, surrounded by cameras and officials on motorbikes. That prevented me from warning her where the hat was, and there was no way she was going to see me, let alone hear me. I ran towards her behind the spectators, jumping, waving and screaming 'Hat ahead, hat ahead ... !' It was to no avail. I saw her running past the hat. She had missed it.

Suddenly she jerked to a halt, bent down and reached for the hat on the road just behind her. But when she came back up, she stopped abruptly and clasped at her hamstrings, which you could almost hear cramping up. For a moment, she stood on the road, bent over, legs apart, unable to move. The crowd went quiet. Then Erin started to shuffle, with short awkward strides, stiff-legged.

'Oh, my god,' I thought. 'Let this not be the end of her race.' Paula Newby-Fraser swept past, not even giving Erin a glance. The crowd started to yell encouragements. After what seemed an eternity, but in reality was probably less than a minute, Erin started jogging, hesitantly at first, but at least she was moving. I tried to run with her, behind the row of spectators, but got trapped in the thick crowd.

I saw her limping up the hill towards the turn onto Queen K Highway at the same time Sylviane came past, ready to pounce. For a long time, there was no news. Spectators were not allowed on the run course outside of Kona. Ien and I were too nervous to find an air-conditioned tearoom for a cold drink and to bide some time. We kept staring up the road, like cows waiting to be milked, knowing full well that the action was not going to come for a while.

Finally, an update from the halfway point of the run filtered back. Paula was 1st, with a slender lead over Sylviane and Erin a couple of minutes back. Relief – she was still in the race. On their way home, all the attention was on Paula and Sylviane, by then running shoulder-to-shoulder. They ran together and slowed down together at the drink stations, where they walked together, almost arm in arm, not breaking back into a run until the other did, as if in an unspoken truce.

All the time, unnoticed, Erin was creeping closer, not by running faster, but by running rather than walking through the aid stations. At the 20-mile aid station, six miles from the finish, she was only 50m behind. At the next aid station, Paula and Sylviane suddenly realised the danger looming up behind them. Sylviane looked back and panicked. She started running halfway through the drink station. Paula, still busy pouring drinks down her throat, reacted a fraction later and started running, then hesitated and slowed down for another walk.

This time it was Erin's turn to sweep past without giving Paula a look. The distance between Sylviane and Erin stayed at 50m until the next aid station. For Sylviane, the drink station walk was too much ingrained in her system and she was unable to adjust. Coming out of the station, she found herself running shoulder-to-shoulder not with Paula, but with Erin. Almost inevitably, she had to let Erin go at the next drink station. She didn't even try. And that was the race.

Hawaii and beyond: A remarkable career

Erin had achieved what she set out to do four years earlier. Her 1987 victory in Hawaii was one of the highlights of a remarkable career. She won the Commonwealth Games Triathlon held in February 1990 in Auckland, New Zealand, in front of a large and ecstatic home crowd. She had not initially intended on competing – at the end of what had been a long hard 1989 campaign she was tired of racing. She did it at the request of her greatest fan, her father, who wanted her to do it for her country. Far from peak fitness, she pulled off the win against a stellar field, relying purely on her grit and determination.

Erin was victorious again at the Hawaii Ironman World Championships in October 1990. During her 10-year triathlon career, she competed in 11 ironman races, winning nine and coming 2nd twice. In addition to her two World Ironman titles, she won two world titles in the short distance event and four over the long distance in Nice. She also won the duathlon world championships twice. Her 10 world championship titles spread over the different events make her the most versatile and successful female triathlete in the history of the sport.[2]

There is another, less well-known side to Erin. Besides the uncompromising and fearless attitude for which she was known during her triathlon career, she also inherited her mother's strong sense of social justice. In the first decade of triathlon, prize money for women was often less than for their male counterparts. Erin led the fight for equal prize money. She urged her fellow competitors to boycott races with unequal prize money between the sexes. She led by example, slating the race organisers publicly for their sexist rulings.

Often this was to her detriment, as generally it concerned races that did have decent prize money, even if it was less for women than for men. The women were not united; some fell for the temptation of a major race where the outcome was not a foregone conclusion. But Erin didn't budge. She was the most dominant female triathlete on the planet at the time and gradually got her way. Her stand has contributed to the fact that today all sanctioned races have equal prize money between men and women.

CHAPTER 2

GROWING PAINS

What if there is a war, and nobody turns up?

April 1970, Groningen. I was 17, in my final year of high school, and it was one of those late-winter Sunday afternoons when the week can't make up its mind whether to start or finish. My father was chasing me around the dining table, but, while the occasional wintry sunbeam danced playfully around us, this wasn't a game. My father was in very real and hot pursuit of me, as a result of a tense discussion that had quickly got out of hand.

The time had come to confront my father with my decision to refuse the call-up to military service. In 1970 a two-year stint in the Royal Dutch Army was still compulsory, a sacrifice expected of every self-respecting and upstanding young Dutch male. But this was also the era of the Flower Power movement, anti-war demonstrations and John Lennon's 'Give Peace a Chance'.

Being a conscientious objector in The Netherlands had serious repercussions. Depending on the basis for your objection, it might mean two years of community service at best, and at worst a prison sentence. Arguments based on religious grounds had a good chance of success, but to me religion was (and still is) a mystery and the cause of too many wars. I had decided to be true to myself and put the doomed case of 'peace by abstention (no armies, no wars)' to the military tribunal and accept the consequences, whatever they were. 'What if there is a war and nobody turns up?' was a quote popularised in the 1960s to protest against the Vietnam War. It resonated with me and I was going to use it in my defence.[1]

When the time came to announce my decision to my father, I expected him to question the wisdom of my intention to boycott the army. But instead of a clearly stated and reasoned opinion he unleashed a tsunami of fury that took me completely by surprise.

Like many of his generation, my father, Nico, had never talked about World War II. Over time, however, I learned a bit more about his wartime experience. Holland was occupied by the Germans from 1940 until 1945. My father was a medical student at the outbreak of the war. He refused to sign allegiance to Germany, which would have allowed him to carry on with his studies. Instead he went into hiding. He was eventually caught and spent some time in a prisoner-of-war camp in Holland. He escaped transportation to a German concentration camp through 'a stroke of luck', when he fell ill with typhoid fever and was declared too sick to make this usually fatal journey. He managed to escape from the camp's hospital and served the remainder of the war years as a member of the Dutch Resistance.

During the war years there was a movement in Holland to promote peace through non-resistance. People who belonged to this group identified themselves by wearing an insignia resembling a broken rifle, but the majority of the population considered these pacifists to be pro-German. That was my father's experience of peace movements and it did me no favours.

Last but not least, the 1960s and 70s were the years of the Cold War between Russia and the United States, with Europe the designated battleground. My father was convinced the Russians were coming, an argument he later used to support my decision to migrate to New Zealand.

When I revealed my convictions to my father that Sunday afternoon, it didn't take me long to wake up to the realities of his world, which did not include having a 'coward' for a son, a view he put to me succinctly while he advanced, fists raised, ready to deal me a hiding, or at least very much giving that impression. Although I was very fit, true to my convictions I'm a lover and not a fighter. More importantly, my father had been a Dutch student boxing champion, another good reason for me to seek refuge behind the safety of our large dining table. He might have been stronger than me, but I was fitter, faster and more agile. Whenever he got too close for comfort, I would shove one of the dining chairs in between us and dart away to the other side of the table.

We continued our 'debate' during the chase, with me accusing his generation of ruining the world with wars, paranoia and capitalistic greed, and him calling me a coward, a weakling and a member of the broken rifle brigade. Meanwhile, my mother, Hanni, was quietly present in the background. She stood in the kitchen, which was separated from the dining room by a large breakfast bar. She didn't interfere at any stage, but I'd like to think she was keeping watch.

I had learned to avoid confrontations with my father. This one was unexpected and rather ferocious. I managed to dodge the hiding and escape to my bedroom, shaken up, but with my beliefs intact; his response had only strengthened my resolve and my abhorrence of violence, physical or verbal.

Family business

I was born in 1953, the second of five children and the only boy. The home in which I grew up was a typical Dutch narrow, multi-storey canal house in Groningen, in the north of Holland. It was one in a row of many, all attached and all similar. A small area in front of the house was separated from the footpath by a low, solid iron railing against which to lean your bike. My father's medical practice occupied the ground floor. Above, a small balcony on the first floor stuck out from the kitchen. Beside that, two large windows indicated the living area. Smaller windows fronted the house on the second and third floors, where the bedrooms were.

You had to crane your neck to see the third-floor window, which was my bedroom. Through a small window in the loft of the house, I could clamber onto the steep roof and lower myself down on the gutter marking the separation between our house and the one next door. This was an ideal hiding place. Or so I thought when a friend and I, in our early teens, were secretly smoking our cigarettes there. One day a hawk-eyed patient of my father's spied us puffing away, perched high above the street between the two roofs. I still remember the hiding I got. I haven't touched a cigarette since.

My father had been a chain-smoker until his early forties, when he quit overnight after reading in the British Medical Journal one of the first research articles published on the link between smoking and lung cancer amongst doctors. For the rest of his life, to pacify his craving for cigarettes, he would suck on *pottertjes* – little round liquorice bullets that burned a hole in your tongue and made your eyes water.

My father was imposing, tall and lean. He had a long face, small eyes, a substantial nose, full lips and prominent ears. His short hair was immaculately combed and firmly stuck to his head with a decent amount of Brylcreem, as was the custom in those days; its side-parting was straight as a ruler, never deviating from its position. His dress code was equally immaculate: always a suit and tie. These features and habits were nothing extraordinary in and of themselves, but the combined effect resulted in a stern appearance that he must have felt befitted a man of his standing. It was not until after his retirement that my father slowly lost the Brylcreem habit, and allowed some softness to creep into his facial expressions, revealing his mellowing character.

He had been brought up by a strict disciplinarian father and three elder brothers. His mother didn't contribute much to the upbringing of her children, as she was deaf and of a sickly constitution, and she died at a relatively young age. His three brothers had all followed in my Opa's[2] footsteps by studying engineering at the University of Delft, and it seemed inevitable that my father was destined for the same path, but they sensed his reluctance and spoke up for him. Thanks to their intervention, my grandfather allowed his youngest son to study medicine.

My mother provided the glue that held our family together. Her disposition might best be described as a subdued cheerfulness. Combined with an even temperament, this stood her in good stead to face the trials of life that came her way. During World War II she was a medical student at the University of Utrecht, but she never spoke about this time.

After she died, in 2010 at the age of 90, my sisters and I found six volumes of notebooks concealed behind a row of books, diaries she had kept between 1939 and 1946. Suddenly her story, which she had hidden from us for all those years, was there before us, a grim treasure. She wrote matter-of-factly and with a clarity and directness belying the emotions she must have experienced at the time, although you also sense carefulness and a reluctance to go into detail in case she is found out. My mother always carried with her a hint of suspicion and now I understood why.

She did not have an easy war. During the famine of 1944, known in Holland as the 'Hunger Winter', she would ride a single-gear pushbike with bare-rimmed wheels over long distances, from the city where she lived into the countryside, to find food for her starving family. On the way, she used to spy on the German military positions for the Dutch resistance. A woman on a bike, a basket with food strapped on the back – the errand provided her with a cover of sorts, but the heart-stopping road-blocks and questioning must have been terrifying.

There is mention of a brief affair with a pastor at a Dutch Reformed Church. It didn't last long, as the requirement for her to attend church not once but twice every Sunday soon became too much for her.

Like my father, she also refused to sign allegiance to the Germans. The many students and lecturers who did not comply with the Germans' conditions organised their own underground classes, and my mother writes about secret lectures in private homes while windows rattled from the frequent bombings. Nurses were not bound by the same requirements, however, so as an enrolled nurse my mother was able to gain valuable practical experience.

She met my father some years after the war. They were both interns at the same hospital, he in internal medicine and she in paediatrics. One day, my mother fell ill and my father would visit her daily and peel fruit for her. She fell for this simple gesture, and soon they were married.

My mother balanced her duties to her husband and the care for her five children with keeping the books for the practice. She also often counselled patients when they rang in distress about something or other, a task my father gratefully left to her. She was called in when the practice nurse was ill or absent, but that was never a success and those were the only times when I sensed marital strain.

Whenever I needed assistance with science-related homework, my mother would send me off to a good family friend living a few houses down from us. Her own interest lay in languages, and in French, English and Dutch literature. German she did not touch. She happily read the books on my compulsory reading list and wrote summaries of them that I subsequently copied out and handed in at school. As a result my marks were rather good; surprisingly neither I or my mother felt any guilt about this.

My father's unpredictable temper threw a dark shadow over our upbringing. It seemed to be fuelled mostly by stress and alcohol, both of which there were in plenty. But they were not the only catalysts. My older sister Joke was a frequent source of provocation. She challenged my father fearlessly during many a discussion about his plans for her future, and their heated confrontations spoiled countless family dinners. He wanted her to study law at the University of Leiden, the most distinguished but also the most conservative university in Holland. Joke had no intention of complying with his wishes and in the end they compromised:

she would study law, but in Amsterdam. Once there, within no time she switched to social sciences. My eldest sister was (and still is) a smart operator.

My sister Lida, who was born in 1956, a couple of years after me, was the perfect baby who never cried, but by time she was three years old my parents suspected that all was not right. Gradually she started to show signs of a puzzling but disturbing behaviour disorder. There was no definitive diagnosis, but she was subject to wildly uncontrolled screaming attacks and acts of self-mutilation which would later be classified as a severe form of autism. Her bedroom had no windows and had to be stripped of all accessories and furnishing except for a single bed against the wall. When Lida was suffering extreme bouts nothing helped except 'time out' in her room, but it was a desperate and ineffective measure; it could take hours for her to calm down, and her piercing cries of anger and despair could be heard throughout the house. It was a wretched situation for Lida, but also for my parents, my other sisters and me. We loved her, and we were all affected by her traumatic screaming and self-harm. Looking back, I feel my father had given up hope and was in a state of denial; my mother did her best with little support. Lida's outbreaks became so severe that when she was 12 she had to be admitted to an institution.

My parents meanwhile tried to have another son, and in their attempts they produced two more daughters – Greet and then Nicolette. These sisters would later combine forces in rowing and went on to win a silver medal in the double sculls for Holland at the Los Angeles Olympic Games in 1984.[3] Greet was the engine, and lightweight Nicolette provided the passion.

From pitch to pool

As a young boy all I wanted to be when I grew up was a professional soccer player. My practice pitch was the size of a postage stamp but that didn't stop me. The yard at the back of our house consisted of a paved area leading to a bike shed and a tiny patch of grass; this was enclosed by a wooden fence on two sides and a hedge on the third. I spent hours there developing my soccer skills, kicking the ball endlessly at the wooden fence, though I was challenged constantly by the thorny roses that grew all the way up to the top – these were my opponents, a formidable team combining attack and defence in one. My teammates were the thorn-free patches in between the roses, gaps that were sparse in summer, more generous in winter.

Thanks to this relentless practice I achieved a level of precision worthy of Holland's top striker, but even so, eventually the roses always won, their victory heralded by the hiss of the deflating soccer ball. To delay this result for as long as possible became my main objective. I appealed to my mother to get rid of the roses or replace them with a less hostile plant, but strangely enough she ignored me. I had no more luck with my father, who decided that hockey was a more honourable game than soccer and better suited to my development as a gentleman. I flatly refused. Hitting a ball with a stick when you have perfectly good feet seemed like a criminal waste to me.

Sometimes during the holidays I went to the swimming pool to clown around with my friends. I became an avid spectator of the training sessions executed by the swim squad who took over the pool following public hours. I would watch them from the balcony, fascinated by the incredible ease with which they carved rhythmically through the water. The coach would shout out the orders, and the streamlined underwater shadows would push off against the wall for the next however-many lengths of the pool.

If I couldn't play soccer, this was what I wanted to do. I begged my father to let me join the swimming club. He said he wanted to meet the coach first. The coach must have made a favourable impression, as I was given permission to give it a try. My focus shifted from playing soccer for Holland to becoming a national swimming champion.

At the age of 14, I was one of the older swimmers in the squad, but initially spent most of my time right at the back of the slow lane. Being the slowest is no fun; you get less rest than the faster swimmers, but you need more. It had all looked so easy from the balcony. Giving up was not an option though, as I had invested too much in convincing my father.

One of my goals was to swim the 100m freestyle faster than a minute. It took me four attempts to achieve it. On three consecutive occasions I swam 60 seconds flat, not one tenth of a second faster or slower. I couldn't believe it, and started to suspect that the timekeepers (electronic timing was still to come) were conspiring against me. At the third attempt, the coach and several spectators clocked me in at 59.8 seconds and I was elated, until the official result once again came up as 60 seconds. I was ready to murder the timekeeper, who was the father of one of my rivals. Soon after that I clocked an official 59.8, but I would never swim faster. Instead I ended up drifting towards the sport of water polo.

Air time

Not long after the dining table incident when I declared my refusal to join the army, my father announced that for my school holidays he had enrolled me in a parachute-jumping training course held on

Texel, one of the islands off the northern coast of Holland. It was an obvious ploy to endear me to some of the adventurous activities the army had to offer. I did not mind, as parachute jumping sounded pretty cool to me.

I biked from home to Texel, a distance of more than 100km. That includes a 35km stretch across the infamous Afsluitdijk, a feat of Dutch engineering ingenuity from the 1930s that divides the sea from a large inlet, now called the IJsselmeer. The Afsluitdijk finally tamed the seas that so often threatened to, and sometimes did, flood large parts of the central coast lowlands.

When I arrived on the island, I discovered that the course was a paramilitary training school attended by soldiers of the Dutch army. God knows how my father had managed to enrol a civilian junior. I was assigned a little tent of my own, while the soldiers shared. I learned from one of the instructors that the minimum age to get your jump certificate had just been lowered to 17, my age at the time.

As the youngest and the odd one out, I was totally ignored by the other half a dozen men enrolled in the course. It was a difficult five days. First we were taught the intricacies of folding a parachute – a very precise business; get it wrong and the consequences can be horrendous. On the first day, one of the instructors showed us a parachute with a faint red bloodstain on it – the result of a poor folding technique, he informed us. We all went very quiet. The policy was that you jumped with a parachute folded by someone else.

We practised our landing technique by endlessly jumping sideways from a small box – very easy and, as I soon learned, very different from the real thing.

The plane used for our jumps was a little Cessna that was missing one of its side doors. The pilot, two students and an instructor fitted into it with difficulty. To prepare for the jump, you were required to step outside onto the wheel of the plane, holding onto a bar that connected the wing above you to the body of the plane. This was the part of the jump I came to dislike the most. Once, the pilot omitted to put the brake on the spinning wheel and when my foot threatened to slip off it I was only just able to recover.

Even with the wheel locked, it was a scary business – standing momentarily outside the plane, attached only by a thin static line, holding on for dear life, jumpsuit flapping violently as the wind tried to tear you away. All the while, you were looking down at a faint, uninviting and distant earth, separated by a dizzying abyss of nothing.

It took only a few seconds before the static line opened the parachute with a reassuring jerk, but it felt much longer. Once the parachute opened, my senses gradually returned. What struck me most about air-time under the huge, coloured canopy was the stillness. The other thing I noticed was how alarmingly small the island was from so far above; so small that it looked easy to miss.

With the ground fast approaching, it was important to keep your wits about you, as the timing of the landing was everything. I never got that right. My landings were nothing like the tidy stuff you see on television, where the parachutists swerve down, touching their feet ever so lightly on the ground, take a couple of elegant dance steps, then come to a halt. To avoid breaking my legs, I generally ended up crashing flat on the ground, which stopped me from taking control of the parachute, an essential requirement after landing. The wind would get hold of it and drag me along the ground through fields full of cowpats, sheep manure and cattle. Barbed wire fences were a particular hazard. I never managed to come anywhere close to our target, a large white cross painted in a field next to the airport. I was happy to land anywhere but in the sea surrounding the island. Sometimes I managed to hitch a ride back to the airport with a local farmer, but on other occasions it was a long walk back.

The pilot flying the little plane was a stunt pilot in his spare time. He took great delight in doing a few tricks on the way up, which for most of us was a good incentive to get out when our time came to jump. He kept his best trick for last. He returned to the airport by stalling the motor and dropping the plane, nose down, falling like a stone out of the sky. Just when it looked inevitable it would bury itself into the ground, he restarted the engine and pulled back up. If we refused to jump that was what awaited us. As a consequence, once we had climbed on board the plane, the compliance level for jumping was high.

We needed eight jumps to get our certificate. For most of the week we were waiting for windows in the weather and I managed only three jumps between the Monday and Thursday. I had to do the remaining five jumps on the final day. They say energy spent during one jump is equivalent to eight hours of hard labour. I certainly experienced every jump as a major life event. The weather that last day was still marginal, but the instructors decided to push on anyway, as they were keen to see us succeed.

On the first jump of the day I was second to go. I waited for the first guy to get in position, but with one foot on the wheel he hesitated. He turned back to the instructor with a terrified look in his eyes and indicated he wanted to get back in. The instructor didn't think twice: he put a boot into the soldier's stomach, sending him hurtling into space. One of the things that had been hammered into us was: once you are committed you cannot go back.

The instructor looked more upset than angry, and indicated to me that it was my turn. I stepped out of the plane and jumped. It was one of my better attempts – we were rated on push-off, body position and landing. Funny how sometimes we can take comfort from other people's fears and thereby lessen our own.

Next day, I set off for home on my bike. I was absolutely knackered, physically and mentally, and my multiple bruises – including some on my backside – made cycling painful. To make matters worse, the wind had not abated and was blasting in my face as I crawled back across the Afsluitdijk. I made it to Leeuwarden, 65km from home, and I could go no further. I parked my bike at the train station and, with no money for a ticket, hid in the train's toilet for the duration of the journey.

The things we do for love

Apart from some innocent flirtations within the swim squad, there wasn't much romance going on in my late teens. Our parties were rather tame by today's standards, with parental control in the background, no alcohol or cigarettes, at best a bit of close-up dancing or even an awkward kiss. Generally, we rode our bikes back to our respective homes on our own, well before midnight, since training awaited us at six o'clock the next morning.

Despite these constraints I found the love of my life. Her name was Ina (Ien – pronounced 'Een') van der Tuin. I suddenly noticed her during one of those early morning training sessions, courtesy of the wonderful new invention of the swim goggle. I 'goggled' her underwater and she gradually replied in kind, and that was it.

A couple of things made the blossoming romance tricky. I was 19 and she 16 (nearly 17). More of a concern was the fact that her father was the swimming coach. Courting the daughter of your coach is definitely high risk. I had to move carefully. I decided to befriend her older brother, Poul, who was also in our squad.

Poul had an obsession with reptiles, in particular snakes. He kept them in terrariums in his bedroom. I didn't much care for reptiles, but pretended to take an interest and asked if I could see his collection. He was eager finally to be able to share his passion with someone, since most people kept well away.

Once in Poul's inner sanctum, I understood why: I watched in horror as a snake devoured a whole live mouse, which Poul had knocked unconscious with a flick of his finger. In addition to witnessing such barbaric acts I had to sit patiently, visit after visit, through lectures about the life cycles of corn, king, gopher, garter and rattle snakes, until I asked one too many times after his sister and he finally figured out the real reason for my visits.

He had a good laugh at my expense and was happy to act as my shield for a while, until his old man was used to seeing me around the house and it dawned on him that his daughter and I were dating. Poul and I are still best mates today. His snake collection now occupies a purpose-built shed the size of a double garage.

Medicine v PE

My father was a gastroenterologist, a specialist in diseases of the digestive system. He was one of the pioneers in that particular branch of medicine in the Netherlands and this gave him the opportunity to make his mark. He was good at his job and was known for his thoroughness in pursuit of a diagnosis.

Because of his reputation, his patients were happy to subject themselves to the terrors of his ways. By terrors, I mean not only what would today be considered crude methods of investigation – including probing the digestive system from either end, or, if you were unlucky, from both ends, with fairly sizeable rigid tubes – but also his brusque bedside manner.

I was confronted with both from an early age. Each morning, to get to my bike from the garden shed I would sneak along the corridor on the ground floor, passing my father's consulting rooms. Through the thin walls I could hear the muffled but nevertheless unsavoury sounds that go with instruments being used to probe digestive and secretory orifices. Sometimes this was accompanied by distressed protestations from the patients, but more often the process was punctuated by impatient instructions barked by my father. It was an experience I never got used to, and it made for an unsettling start to the day.

My father often worked until late at night in his consulting room. One evening, when I arrived home from water polo training, he called out to me to come and see him. 'Son, we need to have a talk.' I sat down on the seat on the other side of his desk, normally reserved for patients. He eyed me up for a short moment. 'You are in your final year of high school. Have you thought about what you want to do next?' I relaxed, as I had anticipated this discussion and thought I was well prepared.

'I'm going to study physical education,' I said firmly. 'I've made some preliminary inquiries and I should get accepted.' I was determined not to show any sign of doubt. There was an awkward silence as my father's eyes narrowed and his face hardened. 'I think you should study medicine, son. You will have a lot more options in life.'

I shuddered at the thought of becoming like him. A doctor – over my dead body, I thought, but was not brave enough to say it. 'I want to do PE,' I managed, but my confident stance was wilting under his stare. He lowered his head, deep in thought, and played with his reading glasses, swinging them between his fingers. I held my breath and sat up, ready to escape. In these situations, I had learned that his reactions could be unpredictable. At least he was sober. He slowly looked up, his face clear of tension. 'Okay, we will do a deal. You do medicine first and then, if you still want to do PE, you can.' With these words ringing in my ears, I was dismissed.

Medical school, 1971–1978

Unlike many of my fellow students I didn't find medical school intimidating. Perhaps it was thanks to my background, having grown up in a medical household, or perhaps it was because medicine was not my first choice of study.

At our first lecture, 400 of us squeezed expectantly into a small lecture theatre where we were immediately challenged by the professor to have a close look at our neighbour, because 'One of you will not be here next year.' The first year's expected attrition rate was 50%. There was room for only 200 Year Two students. My neighbour looked at me wide-eyed. I glared back at him as if to say, 'It won't be me, buddy', and the challenge was laid down. I worked hard to make sure I made the cut.

Once admitted to medical school you don't have to be super smart to get to the end. You just have to be prepared to work hard and memorise all sorts of relevant and less relevant facts. I would cram those into my head in the weeks before an exam, then instantly forget them almost overnight, as if to make room for the next lot. Initially this worried me, but I learned that as long as you know where to find the information again when you need it, it does not matter.

Instruction in bedside manner was not in the curriculum. Once we hit the wards for our practical experience we were confronted by a strict hierarchy: the professors and consultants at the top, followed by the registrars and nurses; the medical student was at the bottom of the heap, together with the patient. The daily ward round was a ceremony to behold, a procession of white coats led by the professor and consultants, with the registrars and charge nurse following at a respectful distance and the medical student taking up the rear, pushing a trolley stacked high with patient files. The group would gather at the foot of each bed to discuss 'the case', muttering amongst themselves in their medical language in a way that excluded and depersonalised the patient. Sometimes, without warning, the learned professor would press his (in those days professors were generally male) stethoscope against the patient's heart, lungs or abdomen with much umming and ahhing but no comment, then move on to the next bed, leaving the patient in a heightened state of anxiety. I would often sneak back to see them after the ward round to explain as best I could what had been discussed.

Most patients seemed vulnerable, consumed by fear of what might be wrong with them, and often thinking the worst. They looked to the doctor for guidance. I learned that more often than not the patients' symptoms did not match those neatly ranked in the textbooks under the different syndromes and illnesses, and that many of the answers to diagnostic puzzles could be found within the patients themselves – you just had to talk to them. I became intrigued and I liked the interaction with the patients. Perhaps I could have a future in this profession after all. I started to see my upcoming career as a privilege rather than an obligation, even if the responsibility which came with the privilege at times felt overwhelming.

Water polo was my sport during my student years and was a good antidote to the pressure of medical school. It's a tough sport. Someone once said that rugby players play rugby because they're not strong enough to play water polo. My own guess is that they just don't float well. We trained twice a week and played games at the weekend. We had a good team and made it to the national first division, which meant we had to crisscross the country every second weekend for our away games. To pass the time on the train the team would play cards, while I took myself off somewhere quiet and got my study books out.

〉〉〉

In the final year of my medical training my father urged me to sit in during his consultations so that I could learn from him. At first I resisted, but by then I had been living away from home for some time and my childhood memories of the unsettling noises from his consulting rooms had faded, superseded by an admiration I'd developed during my studies for his clinical acumen. In the end I relented. I lasted half a day.

I had become used to the dreadful bedside manner of the majority of medical specialists, who were often rude and inconsiderate to their patients, with the odd exception. If I still harboured any hopes that my father might be one of those exceptions, they were quickly shattered during that clinic. I sat through the consultations feeling acutely embarrassed and casting apologetic glances at the patients, who seemed bewildered by my father's impatience and his interrogative approach to taking their medical history.

The last patient of that morning's clinic, newly referred by his general practitioner, presented with lower abdominal pain. My father, who was by now running late, curtly told him to take off his pants and get onto the examination couch on his hands and knees, whereupon without warning he inserted a rectoscope of fearsome dimensions. The man reacted instantly. 'That's not for me,' he said, detaching his backside from the device, putting on his pants and disappearing out the door, leaving my father momentarily stunned, and still holding the offending instrument at butt height.

I was astounded and secretly impressed by the patient's daring. With bated breath I waited for my father to erupt. But he merely shrugged his shoulders, handed the instrument to the nurse without a word, and went upstairs for lunch, while I made myself scarce.

I did learn a lot from observing my father's clinical practice, but not in the way he'd intended; it was a lesson in exactly how not to treat your patients. In my experience over the years I have found that kindness can be a most effective therapeutic tool. It does not take much effort and gains the trust of the patient, which is of tremendous value alongside technical and clinical knowledge.

Firewood

Much against his wishes, my father retired at 65. That was the law in Holland at the time, so he didn't have a choice, but it did give my parents the opportunity to visit us after we had emigrated to New Zealand, which they did several times.

During those visits, without too many words needing to be said, my father and I were able to develop a delicate state of mutual understanding and respect. He enjoyed seeing me leave early in the morning with my doctor's bag, and particularly approved of the times when I came home late, exhausted. If he'd taught his children anything, it was that you must work hard and whatever you do, make sure you do it well. For him, working long hours was an unquestionable part of that.

Even after his retirement, he applied that rule to everything he did, and sawing and chopping up firewood became his favourite pastime. I made sure to have the chainsaw and axe sharpened before my parents came to stay, as during those three weeks he would manage to provide us, and our neighbours, with enough firewood to last the winter.

One day we hosted some friends for a barbeque. My mate Neil was trying to make polite small talk with my father and asked him what he did with his time now he was retired. My father – who was not a great linguist – took some time to answer, and frowned with effort as he searched for the right words.

I was standing close by, listening discreetly and ready to come to his aid. But there was no need for that. He looked relieved, pulled his shoulders back and declared that he worked with wood. To which Neil answered: 'Ah, interesting, and what do you make?' My father looked puzzled, trying to work out why Neil would ask such a question. Then he understood, and his face cleared as he cried out in triumph: 'Firewood!'

My father died suddenly at the age of 76. His health had been fragile for a while. A malfunctioning heart affected him more than he cared to admit and he was quickly losing his strength. 'The wrapping is still good but the content not so' was his standard answer when people asked him how he was. He took a concoction of tablets for his heart, high cholesterol and blood pressure, which he felt gave him the all-clear to keep enjoying the good life –

including gourmet meals and plenty of wine. My father was not much of a one for lifestyle medicine.

>>>

My mother lost her sunny disposition for a long time after my father's death. She explained that she felt only half alive, but after a couple of years she'd regained her cheerfulness.

She was fiercely independent, and concealed her decreasing mobility, her failing memory and her emotions with the aid of a walking stick, a notebook and a 'stiff upper lip' (a discerning observer would notice her lips pursing ever so slightly whenever emotions threatened to break through). 'Good enough,' she would answer steadfastly when we asked after her wellbeing during her later years. Her grey-blue eyes would smile out at you from behind spectacles of the style favoured by the Queen of England, and she would quickly change the topic of conversation.

Her secret to life, she confided to me, lay in the simple fact that she had no expectations. In addition, she had perfected the art of enjoying the little things, like the chattering of birds, a blooming flower, clouds drifting by, a good book, a phone call, or a visit from one of her children, a glass of port or some nice music. I inherited my mother's passions for classical music and books. 'John, what would the world be without them?' she would say. I agree: literature for the mind and music for the soul, and, of course, exercise for the body. I'm convinced her attitude contributed to her longevity. She attributed her good health to avoiding doctors as much as possible, even if she had been a doctor herself and had been married to one.

My mother lived in her own house on the shores of Lake Paterswolde, which she claimed was the most beautiful spot in the world. She fell and fractured her hip when she was 86, and this left her with an unsteady gait and poor balance, further curtailing her mobility. But the worst aspect for her was that she was unable to get back on her pushbike. When illness finally threatened her independence, fate stepped in and she died peacefully in her sleep. My father had cut and chopped so much firewood in his years of retirement that my mother had benefited from it on a daily basis each winter, and it was fitting that her death, 11 years after his, coincided with the end of the woodpile he had left behind.

Lida

My sister Lida died aged 60 in 2017, in the same institution to which she had been admitted in 1968, though it had undergone many changes for the better. Back then, it was like a prison where patients were kept away from the public and locked up in bare rooms. Today, they live in houses in a setting that is fully integrated with the local population, and they are cared for by compassionate professionals.

Whenever I was in Holland I would visit Lida there. Her face would light up when she saw me, and she would laugh affectionately and call out my name, even if we had not seen each other for years. Soon, though, she would hunch over and disappear back into her own mysterious world.

A breakthrough occurred a few years ago when we discovered that she liked cycling, and from then on we would always take her out for a ride on the tandem or tricycle. It was hard work, as Lida did very little of the actual pedalling, but it was worth it, since it seemed to calm her. For my sister, even in small doses, exercise was medicine, too.

CHAPTER 3
DOWN UNDER

First impressions, 1976

Uncle Chris, my mother's brother, migrated to New Zealand a few years after World War II. He was already halfway there – based in Indonesia, where he served his time in the Dutch army – when he made his decision. He wanted to be a farmer, and there were better opportunities in New Zealand than in his home country. Every year at Christmas he sent us a calendar with pictures of pristine beaches, white-capped mountains and ferocious-looking All Blacks, and mysterious, far-off New Zealand had started to hold an attraction for me.

The perfect opportunity for a visit arose after my fifth year of medical training in 1976, when I had a six-month wait before I could start my final year. I decided to use this time productively by arranging medical electives in Australia and New Zealand. Ien and I were by then going steady, both immersed in our studies – she was majoring in dietetics. We knew that my six months away were going to be a test of our relationship.

I spent the first three months in New Zealand at Auckland Hospital under the supervision of John Cullen, a renowned, no-nonsense orthopaedic surgeon who had been a member of the New Zealand gold-medal-winning hockey team at the 1976 Montreal Olympic Games.

The first few weeks I had a perpetual headache trying to make sense of language, culture and protocol. My English was OK, but it was my second language, so asking patients about their bowel and bladder movements, the intricacies of their family relationships and the exact nature of their pain or complaint was particularly challenging. But I got by, with the help of kind nurses, willing staff, patient patients and understanding senior doctors.

It was winter and it rained a lot. There was little time for sport, but whenever I could get away from the hospital I went for a run around the Auckland Domain. In early spring, I was summoned to play cricket for the hospital team because they were one short. For me cricket was as baffling as religion. I didn't understand the rules of the game and was flabbergasted by the fact that after five days of mostly standing around the field we could end with a draw.

Next stop was Perth and the urology ward at the Sir Charles Gardiner Hospital. While Perth was an agreeable city with an even more agreeable climate, the urology ward was a grim place where the terms dribbling, hesitancy and urgency took on a whole new meaning, and the complex, miraculous workings of the kidney eluded my simple brain.

This time I was invited to complement the rugby team – made up of the New Zealand house surgeon and medical student contingent – for their yearly grudge match against their Australian counterparts.

In Auckland I had watched rugby matches, live and on television, in awe. These were real men; fearless physical confrontation, hit after hit, bone-breaking tackles and neck-wrenching scrums. It hurt just watching. The cricket match had felt almost frivolous; the rugby invitation wasn't something to take lightly. I desperately looked for an excuse but couldn't find one and found myself agreeing. To say I was terrified would be an understatement.

I was put on the wing – the 'safest place', I was informed. I was instructed to stay behind the ball at all times and run like the wind when told. When the ball came my way, I found out how hard it is to catch an oval ball while on the run. I fumbled it, again and again. My combined water polo and soccer skills contributed nothing. When I finally managed to catch the ball, more through luck than skill, I was brutally cut short in my stride by the opposition, who had no mercy for this meek, skinny Dutchman. Before I could say 'Colin Pinetree Meads' I found myself buried under a melee of kicking, yelling and fighting bodies. From that moment on, I chose humility over heroics – fumbling the ball was better than catching it and ending up as fodder on the bottom of a ruck. No thanks to me, we won the game. It was the first event in which I 'represented' New Zealand.

My next placement was in Albany in Western Australia, situated 400km south of Perth, where I grabbed the opportunity to experience general practice for a couple of weeks. 'Can you sail?' was the first question my host GP, Joe Lubich, asked me eagerly, before we had even finished the introductions. I had a Laser, which I sailed on Lake Paterswolde. 'Yes,' I confirmed, 'Why?' Joe had just acquired a small, two-person sailing catamaran and he was looking for a partner to take it out on its maiden voyage. 'Great,' he said, rubbing his hands. 'We'll go out tomorrow.'

The only place you can sail in that part of the world is the Southern Ocean, a different beast from the placid lakes of Holland, where the winds can be vicious, but when you're in trouble there are generally plenty of other boats or shores close by. We launched the catamaran on an isolated beach. It was a beautifully clear day with a light onshore breeze and a gentle swell. We sailed further and further out to sea, and I became uncomfortable when the land was only just visible as a hazy outline in the far distance. Suddenly, the weather changed. The onshore wind turned to offshore in a matter of minutes and quickly gathered in strength.

Within no time, the gentle swell whipped into a frenzy of big waves and spray. Dark clouds rolled in out of nowhere and soon we were surrounded by waves the size of multi-storey buildings. They lifted our tiny boat towards the sky like a toy, before dumping it unceremoniously down the trough on the other side. Joe looked petrified and shouted in a cracked voice: 'I can't tack the bloody boat!' Tacking – turning the boat around into the wind – is a difficult manoeuvre in a catamaran at the best of times, let alone in strong winds and rough seas. Every time he tried, the boat stalled and as a result we were gradually being blown towards the South Pole.

'Gybe the bloody thing,' I yelled at him. He looked at me vacantly, so I got up and took the helm. Gybing is the opposite of tacking – you direct the boat downwind with the sail out wide and quickly turn the boat so the sail is being blown in one sweep to the other side of the boat. Voila, the turn is completed. But it's a manoeuvre requiring skill and teamwork, both of which were lacking. The result was an uncontrollable, violent movement of the sail boom across the boat, missing our heads by an inch. When the wind got hold of the sail again, the turn had not been fully completed. The force on the sail was such that one hull was lifted out of the water beyond the point of no return. We were flung into the sea, and the boat capsized.

Within a few seconds, the boat floating upside down with us clinging to the hull, our situation had changed from scary to desperate. We clambered onto the upturned boat and tried to right it. But righting an upside-down catamaran in tumultuous seas is about as easy as walking on water. Joe sat down on one of the hulls with his head in his hands and groaned. 'Not sure what to do,' he admitted, shivering uncontrollably, despite the warm temperature of the water and air.

'Do you think anyone might have seen us in trouble from ashore?' I asked, but when I thought back to the desolate beach from where we'd launched the boat, I knew the answer before he spoke.

'Not likely,' he grunted, wringing his hands.

'Can you swim?' was my next question, although the first rule of the water – never leave your boat in the event of a capsize – flashed through my mind. 'Yes, but ... ' Then he understood and nodded hesitantly. If no one had seen us, our only chance was to try and swim to shore. Without any further discussion, we jumped into the raging seas and headed in the direction of where we thought the shore was. By now it was well out of sight.

Within seconds the boat was gone, and within a few more we had lost sight of each another. I was literally swimming for my life. Every now and then, at the top of a wave, I thought I could see a vague outline of the coast, giving me a glimmer of hope. Next thing I would be down at the bottom of a trough, so deep that it obscured the light. The hopelessness of the situation quickly took over.

I resisted the urge to do away with my life vest in order to swim faster. 'Might be out here for a while, Johnny. You better keep it on.' I kept the waves and wind in my face so I knew I was heading the right way – hoping the wind had not changed direction in the meantime. I suddenly remembered that these waters, close to an old whaling station, were a well-known habitat for sharks.

That thought was too much for me. I rolled onto my back, exhausted, squinting against the light of the sun, which had just ducked out from behind a cloud. For a moment, I relaxed and a feeling of peace came over me. My racing mind eased and came to a standstill of momentary bliss. Then my life flashed before me, all 25 years of it. It might have lasted less than a second or a few minutes, I couldn't say. It felt timeless. I started to swim again, feeling calm and with a sense that everything was okay.

Just then, right in front of me, appeared a small inflatable raft skimming over the top of a wave; the sight brought me as close to believing in divine miracles as I have ever been. I was dragged onboard. I must have made progress, as I could now see the outline of the coast clearly in the distance. The two rescuers asked me if there was anyone else out there with me. I nodded and pointed back out to sea. 'He was behind me,' I said.

We spotted him in the fading light of the day, just when the two rescuers were mumbling that we should get back to shore. Joe was bobbing helplessly in the water. I'll never forget the look of joy and relief on his face when he saw us. We didn't speak, a firm handshake the only acknowledgement between us of what we had been through. The little rescue boat raced back to the beach, carefully navigating the huge surf, and landed with a thud on the beach.

Against the odds someone had seen us, and raised the alarm. Three small inflatable rescue boats were launched, two were beaten back by the surf, one got through. That was lucky. That they then found us in that vast, wild ocean was even luckier, considering it's the same stretch of water where more recently Flight MH370 disappeared. Fourteen planes, nine ships and a submarine – a bit more than one single inflatable – have searched the area in vain for the remains of the Boeing 777.

>>>

The final part of my overseas elective was a stint with the Flying Doctor Service, based in Derby, a small settlement on an inlet in the outback of North West Australia.

The trip there in a little Cessna plane was nearly as terrifying as my ordeal off the coast of Albany. We flew late at night. I was seated next to the pilot who kept nodding off. 'No worries,' I thought, 'there's always the auto pilot'. Then we struck bad weather and thunderous clouds closed in around us. I gently nudged the pilot awake. He adjusted the steering, directing us towards an opening in the black clouds before nodding off again, and I prodded him once more. This ritual was repeated several times. Just when the pilot was starting to get annoyed with me, the weather cleared. He drifted off once again and I didn't bother him after that but stayed wide awake for the rest of the flight.

Derby's hospital was brand new, in stark contrast to the clutter of run-down houses scattered around it. The majority of the population were Aboriginal people. When I arrived I had no idea of their history since colonisation, but soon became aware of the toll it had taken. I was struck by the profound sadness that radiated from the eyes of those I met; they were jobless, demoralised and dispirited. Years of brutal colonial oppression had robbed them of their land, independence, rights and pride – and their health: the European settlers had also introduced a suite of infectious diseases such as smallpox, influenza and measles. The Europeans brought new flora and fauna, too, which led to the extinction or depletion of many native plants and animals on which the indigenous people relied for food. Availability of a 'Western' diet of processed food, much of it high in sugar, and alcohol has resulted in heart disease, obesity, diabetes and alcohol dependency.

With a skeleton staff of consultants, it was up to the medical students to run the day-to-day affairs at the hospital. That included the maternity ward, minor surgery, all emergencies and hospital admissions. Infections like pneumonia, venereal disease and tuberculosis were rife, and kept us busy.

There was not much time for exercise, but in any case the desert-like surroundings and 40°C-plus temperatures were not so inviting. When I did go out for a run in the early morning or late at night, on the rare occasions when the temperature was just tolerable, I wore my stethoscope around my neck for security. The alcohol-fuelled locals, who seemed to brawl continuously, knew that I might have to stitch them up later that night, so they left me alone.

Despite our presence, many Aboriginal patients consulted the traditional healer, whom they trusted more. I could see why. The shiny new hospital seemed like an example of tokenism to me, a half-hearted attempt to provide aid. There was no provision for traditional cultural needs, and I felt this strange environment did not help the patients' recovery, and was more likely to contribute to their demise; for example, the air conditioning benefitted us staff, but babies and children shivered in their cots. It was a hopeless mismatch of two cultures.

Even so, whenever the Flying Doctor Service's small plane arrived at a mission post somewhere in the desert, people would walk for miles to be seen. We would set up a makeshift clinic consisting of a table and a chair under the wing of the plane, but not everyone could be treated there, and we would have to fly some patients back to the hospital. For them the flight was a strange ordeal, adding insult to injury; petrified and sweating profusely they would grip the edge of their seats, deeply suspicious of the metal contraption carrying them through the air. After my own white-knuckled flight to Derby I was well-placed to empathise.

Back in Holland: 'Count me out if it's for violence'[1]

Back in Holland, life was mundane compared to my adventures Down Under. My final year at medical school felt like drudgery.

'You want to come to New Zealand with me?' I asked Ien. We were still together, despite our six-month separation followed by a stressful time preparing for my final medical exams. It didn't take much to convince her.

The choice between Australia and New Zealand was easy. I'd found Australia tough, harsh, dry and monotonous; New Zealand lush, varied and beautiful, with a mild climate. People and populations seem to adapt to and reflect their environment, and to me the Aussies were like their land – tough, plain, ruthless and brash. No wonder they make such ferocious competitors. The Kiwis seemed more subtle, friendly, considerate and compassionate, and I liked the New Zealand way of life with its unique mix of European and Māori culture, the wide open spaces and the stunning landscapes.

There was an added incentive to leave Holland: the matter of military service. The army had granted me a grace period while I was completing my medical training but my time was up. My father was still nursing the hope that the prospect of starting as an officer – the rank immediately assigned to anyone with a medical degree – together with my increased maturity now that I was graduating, would soften my stance towards the army. I was not interested in the officer bit, and my maturity must still have been at rock bottom as I had not changed my mind. I applied for another deferment under the travel and emigration laws, which was granted. One week before our departure, however, I received a letter from the Defence Department informing me that my deferment had been withdrawn. I was to report for duty at a particular time and place.

I called the department to find out more: 'Is there perhaps a war coming up?' I asked. The man on the other end of the line was not amused. He replied tersely that the decision had been made by the computer and it could not be contested. I wrote to the department explaining that I was already committed elsewhere, and mailed the letter on the day we left for New Zealand. I never heard back.

At the time Dutch Customs kept a blacklist of 'defectors' (I was not the only one) for 10 years. When we returned to Holland a couple of times during that period, we made sure we landed at Brussels Airport, cleared Belgium customs, and travelled to Holland by car. Border control between the two countries was non-existent even then.[2]

I had written to all the hospital boards in New Zealand enquiring about vacancies for a house surgeon. Most didn't reply. Some sent a polite note saying they already had a full quota; others sent endless forms to fill in. I had just about given up when a telegram arrived from Mr Graham Smart, the medical superintendent and chief surgeon of Wairau Hospital in Blenheim: 'APPLICATION HOUSE SURGEON ACCEPTED, ACCOMMODATION AVAILABLE, LETTER FOLLOWING,' it read. My return telegram was equally short – 'THANKS POSITION ACCEPTED' – and we booked our tickets.

Wairau Hospital: Lost in translation

Wairau Hospital was a small regional hospital, with about 200 beds, but it was a major employer for the local population. Half the township worked there, the other half were patients, at least that was how it felt; everyone knew each other.

There were five house surgeons, three Kiwis, and me and Wilfried, another Dutchie. The New Zealand house surgeons were our life-savers as they knew the systems and protocols and most importantly were more experienced and knowledgeable than us. Different countries practise medicine in different ways. The Dutch treatment protocols, which I carried around in my pocket, didn't mean much to my New Zealand colleagues; what I had learned and took for granted they questioned, often for good reasons. House surgeons at Wairau were given more responsibility than in the bigger city hospitals, so we got lots of experience.

It was a steep learning curve, and practising as a newly qualified doctor in a language that wasn't my mother tongue added to the challenges. Holland is a relatively small nation, surrounded by much bigger and more powerful countries like Germany, England and France. Learning the basics of English, French and German was therefore part of the curriculum in the Dutch school system. I loved reading in English and I was a fairly competent speaker. So while there was no language barrier there were unexpected hurdles and I often stumbled over them. The first time that a patient died and it was my responsibility to break the news to the family, I searched my brain desperately for a gentle way to tell them. I thought I'd hit on the perfect term, but in fact what I told them was that she had slept in. The Dutch are a notoriously blunt, plain-speaking people, but even so they have an expression similar to the English phrase 'to pass away' – 'inslapen' – and I had directly translated this, not realising it wasn't the same idiom. My English was heavily accented and certain idiosyncracies could cause confusion. On one occasion, after telling patients to go to the laboratory for a blood test (I pronounced it 'labratry') I heard that they were waiting patiently by the toilets.

›››

On my first weekend as a house surgeon I was on duty at the hospital. Early on the Saturday morning I received a phone call from a nurse; it was something about a helicopter and a patient needing to be picked up. I found phone conversations very difficult to understand – words that were already flattened by the Kiwi accent were further swallowed up by an unforgiving telephone line; it might as well all have been in double Dutch. Asking people to repeat every sentence became embarrassing, and much of the time I was left guessing, which led to some awkward situations.

I could hear the thudding roar of rotor blades, and stuck my head around the outside door to see a helicopter landing in the paddock next to the hospital. 'Ah, there you are,' a frantic-looking nurse shouted at me. She pulled me by the sleeve towards the helicopter, pushed a large backpack into my hands, told me 'Everything you need is in here' and disappeared before I could ask any questions.

I was left none the wiser, standing in the middle of a sheep paddock, in a white doctor's coat, stethoscope still around my neck, the backpack in my arms. The pilot gestured from the helicopter for me to get on board. Then he pointed at his head and kept pushing it down, bobbing like a duck, the reason for which I discovered when my head was nearly taken off by the rotor blades. 'So that's why the soldiers in the movies always run towards a helicopter in a seriously bent-over position,' I thought. I hopped in and before I could say 'Hello, and where are we going today?', let alone put my seatbelt on, the helicopter was airborne.

The weather that day was windy and wet, and the helicopter shook violently with every gust. There was too much noise to attempt any conversation. Beneath us appeared a vast landscape of lonely fiords, a giant network of intricate waterways separated by steep, green, inaccessible-looking hills. I gathered that these were the Marlborough Sounds. I had been in the country for a few weeks and I had already been awed by its vastness, but observing this eerie land and seascape from a violent sky was like looking down at a different planet, or at a place at the end of the world. It felt as if we were flying for hours over this endless landscape, the scene partly obscured by patches of grey clouds. All the time we were buffeted in every direction by unpredictable blasts of wind. The helicopter shuddered, and went up, down and sideways, one way, then the other. The white caps of Cook Strait appeared in the distance and I wondered when and where this trip would end. Then, as abruptly as the helicopter had taken off it landed on a small beach somewhere in the outer Sounds. After the din of the motor and the whirring of the rotor blades had stopped the howling of the wind took over.

My relief at being back on terra firma was short-lived. The pilot turned to me. I still didn't know his name. 'You've got 30 minutes to do the job,' he said, 'The tide's coming in'. 'What job?' I mumbled.

He looked at me aghast, 'There's been an accident, please go and see to the patient, hurry up!' and he pointed towards a rough track up a slight raise at the end of the beach. I hoisted the hefty pack onto my back and followed his directions. Someone came running down the track and took me to the other side of the hill where groans were coming from behind an overturned tractor. A farmer had sustained a nasty compound fracture of his thigh bone when his tractor had rolled on top of him. He was very lucky that his neighbour was with him when the accident happened and had raised the alarm. My mind was racing: 'Painkillers, I have to give him something for the pain before we can transport him ... and we also need a splint for his leg ... yes ...'

I unpacked the backpack. Out came a sleeping bag, a first-aid kit, some paraphernalia I didn't recognise, a couple of survival blankets, followed by a range of inflatable splints ... thank God for that. I opened the first-aid kit but the strongest painkiller I could find was paracetamol. Desperately I turned the backpack upside down to see what else I could find and suddenly found what I was looking for, a small box of ampoules amongst which the morphine was carefully hidden. By this time the helicopter pilot had arrived on the scene carrying a stretcher. He hopped impatiently from one leg onto the other, urging me along. 'Come on, doc, we don't have much time, 15 minutes at the most, hurry up or we won't be able to get out'.

With trembling hands I broke the top off the ampoule and in the process cut my finger. 'Shit,' I thought, then, 'Band-Aid, I need a Band-Aid to stop the bleeding'. But Band-Aids were nowhere to be found amongst the chaos of medical aids spread out on the ground. Very quickly everything was smeared with blood, mine not the patient's. In the end I wound my handkerchief around the offending finger, injected the morphine into the by now half-conscious patient and started to rummage through the splints. There was one for the wrist, one for the neck and one for the lower leg, but there was nothing for the whole leg ... 'Bugger' ... I shouted at the helicopter pilot and the neighbour to find a splint that I could use for the farmer's leg.

There were plenty of trees around and they soon came back with a suitable branch of about the right length. By this stage the pilot was beside himself: 'Look,' he said, 'We need to get him to the helicopter now or it will be too late.' I strapped the branch to the leg as quickly as I could and we lifted the patient onto the stretcher. Throughout this mayhem the poor patient had been moaning softly, drifting in and out of consciousness. His groans became louder during the bumpy, uncoordinated dash to the helicopter and climaxed with a scream when the pilot stumbled and fell and we dropped the stretcher. When we arrived on the beach the incoming tide was lapping at the helicopter' skids. The pilot jumped into his seat, 'Quick!' he yelled, while he turned the key of the ignition. With one big heave I lifted the patient up and shoved him onto the passenger seat, a clumsy manoeuvre that caused another agonising scream.

I was still standing on one of the landing skids when the helicopter left the ground. I threw myself on top of the patient who, fortunately for him perhaps, had well and truly passed out by then. I wriggled myself into a spot next to him and quickly turned around to close the helicopter door but I couldn't – his splinted leg was still sticking out. There was no way to get his extended leg, with the end of the branch sticking out well past his foot, into the helicopter, so I held on tightly to the half-open door for the whole flight. When we arrived back at the hospital, me still in my white doctor's coat and with my stethoscope dangling uselessly around my neck, I felt a little bit Superman, a little bit Mr Bean.

But the day was not finished with me yet. That afternoon, still recovering from the morning's adventure, I psyched myself up for the post-match rugby injuries which I had been promised would come in thick and fast.

This was one of the things I had been looking forward to. I had developed an interest in sports medicine and I was keen to reacquaint myself with rugby injuries. I would once again be dealing at first hand with the fractures, cruciate ligament ruptures, dislocated shoulders and concussions that I had seen in Auckland, and which I had been studying since then in the sports medicine textbooks. In Holland the national game is soccer. Compared to rugby, soccer is a gentle game and any violence tends to be confined to the stands. Most soccer injuries are minor strains and sprains, many of which seem to be psychosomatic, judging by the theatrics involved. 'Soccer players pretend to be hurt when they are not, while rugby players pretend not to be hurt when they are' is a quote I've since picked up in New Zealand.

I was ready early that Saturday afternoon to once again attend to some 'real' sports injuries and have them all to myself. I waited, waited and waited. Nothing happened. I saw a toddler who had fallen from a swing, a woman with a bladder infection and an old man who was confused, but no rugby players. The minutes and hours ticked by. Then at 5.30pm all hell broke loose. A bus arrived and a horde of loud, intoxicated rugby players fell out and stumbled into the emergency rooms. They had been to the pub for their 'anaesthetic' before coming to the hospital to have their injuries treated.

It had been worth the wait. I was presented with a feast of lacerations requiring suturing, a dislocated shoulder, a couple of cruciate ligament ruptures, fractures and head injuries. I was in sports medicine heaven even if I was well out of my depth. Little was said, which was good. There was a lot of grunting, but that I understood. The players stoically put up with any treatment I dished out to them. Local anaesthetic or other pain relief was not required in the majority of cases; they seemed to wear that as a badge of honour. 'Welcome back to New Zealand, John,' I said to myself with satisfaction, after I had discharged the last patient four hours later.

Mr Graham Smart

Graham Smart, the Medical Superintendent and Surgeon of Wairau Hospital, was an Englishman who had ruled the hospital with a firm but benevolent hand since 1950. Besides running the hospital he worked as a full-time surgeon and did outpatient clinics, post-mortem examinations, was responsible for the weekly house-surgeon tutorials and also served as a coroner. When he retired in 1980 he was replaced by no fewer than seven managers.[3]

Graham looked like an elf, small in stature with a round belly. His friendly face was just as round, and his bushy white eyebrows and gold-rimmed glasses only partially hid his kind, sparkling eyes. What remained of his wavy snow-white hair clung precariously to the sides of his balding head. He often grimaced or winced, sometimes for no obvious reason, but perhaps because of pain in his leg; in his youth he had suffered from osteomyelitis (severe bone infection), which had required multiple operations and left him with a permanent limp – and all that time in hospital had also sparked his interest in medicine.

A man of few words, Graham was always worth listening to. When he did speak, dispensing wit or wisdom, it was in short bursts, almost as if he was out of breath. When I think of the saying 'brevity is the soul of wit'

I think of him. He had a great sense of humour, which he expressed with a wry smile and a twinkle in his eye.

Friendly he may have been, but when it came to clinical practice he was no pushover. His standards were high, especially where patient safety was concerned. He would not tolerate preventable mistakes and he hauled me over the coals when I prescribed an antibiotic to a patient without checking whether they were allergic to it (they were). One of the more important rules of the Hippocratic Oath is not to harm your patient. I never forgot the dressing down he gave me in front of my colleagues and I've never made that mistake again.

When Graham had first arrived at Wairau he had pushed hard to improve and expand the facilities, and he was a great person to have on your team. Halfway through our year in Blenheim Wilfried and I received a letter from the New Zealand Medical Council informing us that, due to a rule change regarding foreign doctors, our medical registration would not, after all, and as we'd been led to expect, be automatically extended at the end of the year subject to good behaviour. Wilfried and I were not aware of any major transgressions on our parts and had no desire to return to Holland so soon, and we went to see Graham to protest. He called the Medical Council and they confirmed that, yes, the new ruling now applied and, no, there was no process of appeal. Graham could have left it at that. But he didn't. He flew to Wellington and went into bat for us with the powers that be. They relented and Wilfried and I were allowed to proceed under the old rule, which made our permanent registration at end of the year extra sweet.

I also remember Graham for three of his passions: reading medical journals, completing cryptic crosswords and participating in the local repertory theatre, of which he was the president, secretary, scriptwriter, editor and star player. He always carried a medical journal with him wherever he went and he'd read it whenever he got a chance, before scrubbing up for theatre, or while walking along the corridors in the hospital. Every morning around seven he would walk past our house to the hospital with his nose in one of his journals, completely asbsorbed in his reading. I worried that one day he would trip and fall as his gait was quite unsteady, but he never did.

Much later I found out from one of his daughters that concealed within the pages of the medical journal was invariably the script for his next play or a crossword puzzle.

Marlborough Harriers: Quaint customs

Soon after we arrived in Blenheim to start our New Zealand lives proper, late in 1978, I explored the possibility of joining one of the local water polo clubs, only to find out that there weren't any. I briefly considered starting a team, but we would have no opponents unless we were prepared to travel to Christchurch or Wellington. You can't do that every weekend. So, I took up running. It suited my irregular working hours and I soon embraced the space, the solitude and the views all the way to Cook Strait from the tops of the Wither Hills.

It was the time when athletics was flourishing in New Zealand. John Walker ruled the world over the English Mile. Middle distance runners Allison Roe, Rod Dixon and Dick Quax were household names in New Zealand. Harrier clubs were thriving.

It was against this background that I joined the Marlborough Harriers Club. I was not a bad runner, courtesy of a solid aerobic platform from my years of swimming and water polo and the ownership of long levers that helped propel me forward. During my swimming career in Holland, I ran once a week as part of dry land conditioning, and when I competed in the odd local cross country race in the winter months I would invariably take out the 'non-registered athletes' category.

New to the New Zealand way of cross country racing, I turned up for my first club event with the Marlborough Harriers on a beautiful autumn Saturday afternoon in a paddock somewhere close to Blenheim. I worked myself around the course with a sense of awe. It required concentration to master the natural and man-made obstacles as efficiently as possible. It felt pure, almost spiritual – sport in all its simplicity. The other competitors seemed almost irrelevant as I went at my own pace, in my own rhythm, passing others with respect, and not minding too much when others passed me. It was in stark contrast with the tightly organised 'cross country' events held in the cultivated, populated and mostly flat public parks and forests in and around the Dutch cities.

After the race, out of nowhere there appeared a large table, which was soon covered with home-baked cakes, scones, biscuits and other sweet treats. Afternoon tea was served, which struck me as a very English custom, and a rather quaint one, especially when practised out in the whop-whops after a running race. I was delighted. I was also hungry, so I helped myself to some goodies and a cup of tea. It topped the afternoon off nicely.

At the prize-giving a fellow competitor pulled me aside and informed me that I was supposed to have brought a plate. That sounded fair enough to me, so the next week I produced a plate and stacked it up high with goodies. The same competitor must have been keeping a really close eye. Taking me aside again, he said patiently: 'John, when you bring a plate, there's supposed to be something on it, something to share. You need to ask your wife to do some baking. That's the custom.' I nearly choked on my bun, not only out of embarrassment but also at the thought of asking Ien to bake a cake for the Harriers Club. I could just imagine her response, along the lines of: 'Why don't you bake your own bloody cake!' Not wanting to make matters worse, I didn't explain to Busybody that I was not married, given that Blenheim in the late 1970s was still a bastion of conservatism. Germaine Greer's *The Female Eunuch* was only discussed in whispers in dark corners by a few brave revolutionary souls, and cohabitation was severely frowned upon.

On the way to the next club run I stopped at a bakery, bought a nice-looking cake, unwrapped it, planted it firmly on my plate and put some Gladwrap over the top. 'Nice cake, John,' my new friend commented slyly while he took a taste. 'Did your wife bake this?' I mumbled something incomprehensible in response and walked away. It turned out that the cake I had bought was a well-known regional delicacy, only available at the local bakery. It was an embarrassing start to my New Zealand sporting career. From then on I took a packet of supermarket biscuits with me to every race I attended.

>>>

In the winter of 1979 I was selected to compete for Marlborough at the Tasman regional cross country championships. They were held in Okaramio, a tiny settlement halfway between Blenheim and Nelson. We travelled there by bus, a distance of less than 30km.

Blenheim – located in the east at the top of the South Island – is one of the driest places in New Zealand, with a mere 500–750ml of rainfall a year. In contrast, the West Coast of the South Island has the most rainfall, with up to 6000ml a year. The Southern Alps hug the West Coast and stop the bulk of the rain, gathering up incoming weather from the Tasman Sea and hindering its progress towards the east. In the Nelson area, the Alps peter out into gentler hill country, allowing the wet to spread its tentacles further, as far as Okaramio. This is why the yellow, sun-dried hills of Blenheim show little similarity to the lush green landscape that soon greets the traveller going west.

It had rained solidly for a week in Okaramio before the race, and it was still raining when we arrived. West Coast rain is not like the rain most of us know. It comes down in bucket-loads and can do so for days on end. When the bus stopped at our destination, I wiped my hand over the fogged-up window. The roar of the heavy rain on the roof was deafening. What I saw was alarming: rain had turned the paddocks that we were supposed to run around into a lake of mud, water and drowned sheep. No doubt the event will be cancelled, I thought, but there was no sign of that happening. The team manager handed out race numbers and urged us out of the bus to get ready.

'This is crazy,' I said to Kerry Sowman, a teammate sitting next to me. 'Surely the race will be cancelled in these conditions.' Kerry gave me a puzzled look, then laughed and asked, 'Why?' before he got up and out into the pelting rain.

Ten kilometres of energy-sucking mud, knee- to waist-deep river crossings and plenty of dead sheep-hopping later, I crawled over the finish line happy to still be alive. Dennis Patchett won the race – running in bare feet. In finishing that race, I made my first symbolic step into the culture of New Zealand sport, a culture I discovered was steeped in tradition, pride, stoicism and toughness.

On the way home in the bus I said to Kerry: 'So this is how you do it. This is why this small country with so few inhabitants is so good at sport.' Kerry looked nonplussed for the second time that day. He didn't know any different.

An unconventional wedding

Unbeknown to us, prior to our arrival the Marlborough Hospital Board had agonised over where to house this Dutch house surgeon and his 'fiancée'. It had been on the agenda at one of the board meetings, and opinion was divided over whether to station Ien, who was going to work as a dietitian at the hospital, in the nurses' home, and me in the house surgeons' quarters, or to let us 'live in sin' and flat together.

Ultimately common sense prevailed, if only by a whisker, and we were allowed to share a flat. An unplanned consequence of this liberal arrangement was that Ien fell pregnant. In Holland, that wouldn't have raised too many eyebrows, but it did in conservative Blenheim, and in the name of cultural integration we decided to tie the knot. It was a memorable occasion, for more than the usual reasons.

We asked my fellow house surgeon Peter Haeni to be best man at the wedding. Peter had only recently arrived at Wairau Hospital from Switzerland and we had become good friends in the short time we'd known him. Besides being a doctor, he was a qualified mountain guide, and had introduced Ien and me to tramping the tracks of the New Zealand wilderness.

We entrusted Peter with the task of bringing the marriage celebrant to Whites Bay beach in the Marlborough Sounds, where the ceremony was going to take place. The rest of the small bridal party had preceded them and consisted of our new Dutch friends and fellow immigrants Laura and Maarten Reynders and their two young children, and one of the nurses from the hospital who gate-crashed proceedings.

Halfway into the 30-minute journey the marriage celebrant suddenly demanded that Peter stop the car. He got out and looked at the road ahead, winding up the hill towards a bright blue sky. 'You won't get me over that hill,' he announced, looking defiantly at Peter. The celebrant had already expressed his reservations about holding the ceremony away from the sanctity of the church, and he probably saw the hill as a sign from God. He said if he had known about it he would never have agreed to preside over the wedding; he had a fear of heights and expected that he would get dreadfully car sick.

Peter calmly considered the elderly man's pale and anxious face, playing for time and trying to work out a strategy to change his mind. He suggested they sit down. He had the picnic hamper for the wedding celebration in the boot of the car, so how about a drink before he took him back home? The celebrant admitted to a fondness for whisky, and a few drinks later Peter bundled him into the back of the car, where he dozed off as soon as the key was turned. Instead of returning home, though, Peter drove gently up the hill, keeping a close eye on his sleeping passenger in the rear-view mirror.

Meantime, our bridal party was already on the beach and starting to get worried. What if the car had broken down? Had they got the time wrong? Or even the day? Just when we decided one of us should head back to find the missing persons, a cloud of dust became visible in the distance and Peter and his precious cargo arrived. He apologised for the delay and said he would fill us in later: 'Long story, but we're here now.' He opened the back door of the car and the celebrant awoke with a startled look. 'Good heavens, where am I?' Before we could answer, he composed himself, stepped unsteadily out of the car, straightened his jacket and suggested we proceed to the rocky end of the beach for the ceremony.

The otherwise-deserted beach glistened under a stark blue sky, and there was a post-rain freshness in the air, with not a breath of wind. Small waves on an incoming tide unfolded onto the sparkling white sand. Ien looked simply stunning. Her big emerald-green eyes shone with happiness and anticipation and her long, wavy dark-brown hair was adorned with a headband covered with little red roses. The off-white wedding dress was beautiful in its simplicity.

I didn't look too shabby myself. For once I felt comfortable in a suit and tie; they seemed right for the occasion.

The ceremony was a jolly affair. The marriage celebrant, who still seemed a bit tipsy, lost his place, dropped his papers and repeated himself a few times, ignored our instructions to avoid religious references and, in the end, he married us as John and Ginn. 'John, do you take Ginn to be your lawfully wedded wife?' 'Yes,' I said, because I wasn't marrying Ginn, I was marrying the only thing I saw – those wonderful emerald eyes. Before we knew it, Ien and I were frolicking knee-deep in the surf, with pants and skirt rolled up high, glasses of champagne in hand. The celebrant stood on the beach looking on in amazement, slowly sipping his whisky.

After a year in Blenheim, we decided to move on. We were not yet ready to settle down and I was still considering further specialisation. Orthopaedics appealed, but specialising would mean at least four more years locked inside the hospital for 60-plus hours a week, not to speak of the exams to sit and prepare for. With our baby on the way and my budding sporting career about to take off, I decided against it. I did a second house surgeon year at Christchurch and Burwood hospitals before enrolling in the general practice training programme, and Ien juggled motherhood with a part-time job as a dietitian at the hospital.

Christchurch and the New Brighton Harriers, 1980

As soon as we arrived in Christchurch, I joined the New Brighton Harriers, where my running career took a more serious turn. In 1980, the club broke the stranglehold the Auckland clubs had held until then, and gained the unofficial title of 'strongest athletic club in New Zealand'. The accolade came with winning the national road relay championship, and I played a small part in the New Brighton Club's first historic victory.

The club was blessed with an abundance of national- and international-level road and track runners. Olympic steeplechaser Peter Renner, Tom Birnie, Don Greig, Neil Lowsly, Grant McEwan, Rob Mulcahy and Mel Radcliffe were all capable of running 10km in less than 30 minutes. I had qualified for the eighth and final spot on the team in a fiercely contested club race.

That year, the relay went from Wellington to Masterton. I was given lap four, at barely 6km the shortest lap. We were up against the favourite star-studded Auckland teams Lynndale and Auckland University. I ran my heart out, and when I finished my lap found to my relief we were still in contention.

Relays transform an individual sport into a team sport. You get a taste of that wonderful sense of belonging and wanting to do well not only for yourself but also for your mates. It can make you fly. Brent Rollo ran the lap up the Rimutaka Hill, a brutal 6.6km climb to nearly 600m. He did not fly. He got into real difficulty halfway up the hill and slowed to a crawl, losing significant time. He was diagnosed with glandular fever a few days later. It nearly cost us the race.

On the final lap, Tom 'Cannonball' Birnie did the impossible by making up a two-minute deficit with less than 800m to run. Tom was renowned for his lightning finish, hence his nickname, and he didn't disappoint. And so, the club won the first of seven national road relay titles over 10 years. For me, the boyhood dream of becoming a national champion had suddenly and unexpectedly come true.

Uphill specialist

I didn't want to miss out on our title defence the following year, especially as it was a 'home game', the Takahe-to-Akaroa relay.[4] By then I had won the Christchurch King of the Mountains race, during which the selectors (and I) had discovered my ability to run up a hill faster than a scalded cat. I became the team's designated uphill specialist.

Our best runner, Peter Renner, threw a spanner in the works. He was in the lead on his 9.4km fourth lap, but collapsed 400m from the finish. He had only hours before stepped off a plane after returning from a competition overseas. He hadn't felt well, but insisted on running. Now he lay delirious on the side of the road and it became clear he wasn't in any shape to get to the finish of his lap. A message was sent to the next runner on the team, Neil Lowsley, to run back to retrieve the baton from Peter, which cost a considerable amount of time. I was oblivious to the drama, waiting impatiently in Cooptown, ready to tackle lap six, the 6.9km slog up to Hilltop, the saddle connecting Little River with Barry's Bay. I knew there was something wrong when competitors from other teams came past and no New Brighton singlet was in sight.

Finally, a flustered looking Neil appeared and handed me the baton. Puzzled but undeterred, I set to work. I had a job to do. I used other runners ahead of me as magnets, pulling myself up from one to the next. I had practised the route a few weeks before, so I knew the road, the bends, the gradients, where I could push it and where I needed to be careful. I knew that when you think you're nearly there you're not.

Helped by a light southerly tail-wind, I ran the perfect race. I had nothing left when I handed the baton over on the top of the hill to our downhill specialist, Dave Thomas. I wasn't in a good way, crouching on the side of the road, when my mate John Docherty came running up to me. 'John, we're back in second place and you've broken the lap record.'

I had cracked it by a mere two seconds. The record had belonged to a West Coast runner, Eddie Gray, who set the mark in 1968, meaning it had stood for 12 years. As it was, however, we never caught the Auckland University team and finished a disappointing 2nd.

>>>

Five years later, in 1986, I travelled with the team to the North Island again to run the uphill leg of the New Zealand road relay championships. The relay that year went from Morrinsville to Tauranga, across the Kaimai Ranges, a total distance of 83km. A surprise entry was the famous Japanese S&B[5] road-running team, coached by Kiyoshi Nakamura. Toshihiko Seko was their star athlete ('Marathon is my wife and I gave her everything I have,' he once famously said), but all members were successful international road runners.

Nakamura was a great admirer of Arthur Lydiard, the renowned New Zealand coach, whose training principles he followed. In honour of Lydiard, he brought his team to New Zealand for a summer training camp every year for many years. That particular year, they decided to enter the road relay championships as a training run. They put five runners up against New Zealand's top club teams, which had 10 runners per team. That meant each S&B runner had to run two legs of the relay. They chose to run consecutive laps. The team included Douglas Wakiihuri, an up-and-coming Kenyan distance runner. He was going to be one of my opponents running the uphill leg.

By the time I took over the baton for my New Brighton team at the start of lap six, Douglas had already run the previous 8km leg. He was 50m ahead when I set off in pursuit. I reeled the Kenyan in greedily within the first kilometre and soon fell into step with him, running right by his side.

The first thing I noticed was that, despite the fact he had been running at a sub-30-minute 10km pace for some time, he was not perspiring. Neither was he breathing much, as his lips seemed to be closed. After my quick catch-up heroics on the initial flat bit of road, I was well into oxygen debt and we hadn't even started the 4km climb to the top of the Kaimai Range.

Douglas seemed to ignore me completely, his serene face totally relaxed, his gaze fixed on the road ahead. He was very tall. At 184cm I am tall, but he was taller than me. His upper body was still, floating above the rhythmically moving legs, with his feet hardly touching the road. Tiny droplets of perspiration finally started to appear on the dark skin of his forehead and upper lip, like small pearls, the first and only sign of effort. What a contrast it must have been, this perfect running machine, next to my contorting, swaying body, shoulders hunched, panting, grimacing and drenched in perspiration.

Soon, the stinging of the sweat in my eyes and the pain in my legs forced my attention away from my companion towards my inner demons, which screamed at me to slow down. Uphill running is total effort, as you use more muscles than when you run on the flat. Gravity not only pulls you down but also backwards, requiring more force from the muscles to maintain forward momentum. Easing off a fraction results in significant loss of speed compared to running on the flat. It's relentless.

I was 'red-lining it', which is when your body screams out for oxygen, your lungs burn and your legs hurt so badly that you want to lie down and shoot yourself. Then, suddenly, it was all over. Douglas accelerated so fast that he broke the sound barrier, boom. I had no time to react, not that there was anything left in me to react with. The finish line was a short distance up the road and I hadn't seen it coming. He had well and truly out-sprinted me.

The S&B team gradually built a sizable lead which our secret weapon for the final lap, Peter Renner, was unable to overcome. Their final runner was Yutaka Kanai, who had come 7th in the 10,000m at the 1984 Los Angeles Olympics. We still won the national title, as the S&B team was not eligible.

Douglas Wakiihuri went on to win the world marathon title the following year in Rome. He won the silver medal at the Seoul Olympics in 1988 and the gold medal at the 1990 Commonwealth Games in Auckland. He also won the London Marathon in 1989 and the New York Marathon the following year, heralding an era of Kenyan dominance in distance running. The memory of running side-by-side with this future running legend, with no one else in sight except for an occasional hardy spectator, will always stay with me as one of the more poignant moments of my sporting career.

>>>

In 2014, I returned to my old hunting ground, lap six of the Takahe-to-Akaroa road relay, with the aim of breaking the over-60s record – only to find out that there wasn't one. Besides the open record, I already held the veteran 40-plus and 50-plus age-group records, so it only made sense that I would have a go at the record for the geriatric division as well. But the newly introduced over-60s relay finished at the end of lap five, just before the uphill fun starts. I was given a place in the New Brighton Olympic Club's over-50s team so that I could run my favourite lap six once more.

I hadn't run the hill for 10 years and had forgotten what it was like. My legs went rubbery as soon as I hit the hill and my heart and lungs were ready to explode in an attempt to meet the oxygen demands of my failing legs. I realised why geriatrics were being kept away from this heart-busting climb. No competitors had died in all the 74 years this most prestigious of relays had been held, and the organisers were not going to tempt fate by allowing over-ambitious senior citizens, still dreaming of past glory, to expose themselves to the potential risk of cardiac arrest. (But what a glorious death it would be.)

Andrew Davidson came past not far from the top of the hill. The former New Zealand cross country champion was in the lead for his Auckland team in the senior men's race, which had started an hour behind ours. As he passed, he turned towards me and gave a slight bow, a big smile on his face. It was a nice gesture, but I thought: 'Mate, if you can still smile, you're not working hard enough.'

The times I set up the hill from Cooptown to Hilltop over the years have provided me with brutally honest feedback regarding my physical demise over time. In 2014, aged 61, I ran 33 minutes and 52 seconds; when I was 50 it was still a respectable 29:32. Ten years before that, the time was 26:22, just over a minute slower than my senior record of 25:19, set in 1981.

It amounted to an overall decline of 32% in strength-endurance over a period of 30 years. This would not be so bad if the decline were linear, because that would mean I will still run 42 minutes when I'm 90. Unfortunately, as the astute observer will deduce from these numbers, the decline in fitness is exponential. The older you get, the more rapidly you lose it, which means that for me the end must be nigh.

The open record for lap six, which I set in 1981, still stands at the time of writing. It must be one of the longer standing and more obscure records in the annals of New Zealand athletics.

CHAPTER 4

TRIUMPHS AND TRIBULATIONS

The early years, 1982–1985

According to the Americans, the first recorded triathlon took place at San Diego's Mission Bay in 1974. It was organised by the San Diego Track and Field Club as an alternative to the rigours of training on the track. The race consisted of a 5.3-mile run followed by a 5-mile cycle ride and a 600-yard swim. Forty-six athletes finished the race. One was John Collins, who went on to organise the first Hawaii Ironman in 1978.

But the Americans were a bit premature in claiming San Diego as the birthplace of triathlon, as there is evidence that the first triathlons were held in France in the early 1900s. They were called 'les trois sports' – the three sports. The first documented triathlon was held in Joinville-le-Pont in 1902 and consisted of run/bike/kayak. In 1920, the kayak was replaced by a swim, which makes it technically the first triathlon as we know it today. The distances were a 4km run, 12km bike ride and a swim across the Marne River.

The first New Zealand triathlon took place in Auckland in 1979. It was won by Ian Barnett, who had a background as a competitive runner. The Les Mills Fitness Centre, the first facility of its kind in New Zealand, saw the exciting new sport of triathlon as a vehicle to advertise its fitness business. The marketing manager at the time, Phil Briars, organised the event with gusto. The risky concept of combining the three sports of swimming, biking and running immediately took off. The media were intrigued, and participants – initially mainly fitness fanatics from different sports – were drawn to the challenge in great numbers. For years, the self-proclaimed 'Les Mills New Zealand Ironman Championship race' was New Zealand's premier triathlon event.

In those early years, triathlon was simply known as 'ironman', as the format was based on the sole international triathlon event known at the time, the Hawaii Ironman. The 3.8km swim, 180km bike ride and 42km run of the Hawaii Ironman received international acclaim, on the one hand as absolute madness, but on the other as an event that re-set the boundaries of human endurance. It was simultaneously ridiculed and admired (and still is today). The idea of racing in three different disciplines back-to-back – let alone over the official Hawaii Ironman distance – was considered extreme. It was believed the distances of the Hawaii event could be covered only by the toughest of the toughest. Therefore, organisers of similar ironman events all over the world used shorter distances to make it achievable for mainstream fitness lovers.

I had followed this novel event closely for three years from the day that I first watched it on television in 1979. Every year the race was bigger and better, and every year the television coverage increased – and with it my desire to enter the event, as I considered myself well versed in the three disciplines.

Nobody knew yet how to prepare for such an event. There was no information available, so I had to make up my own training programme. With a busy general practice and a young family, I did the bulk of my training in the early hours of the morning, before my family stirred and the city came to life.

Through my experience with the different disciplines over the years, I knew that being fit in one discipline doesn't prepare you for the other two. My training needed to accommodate the requirements of all three sports. I read up on basic training principles for endurance sport and worked out that if I did three or four sessions in each discipline each week I would be 90% fit in all of them, making me pretty competitive. I worked out the only way I could squeeze 9 to 12 sessions into the week was by combining them. I would bike or run to the pool, swim 3km, and then bike or run home. Or I biked to the Port Hills, hid my bike in the bushes, and ran for an hour before biking home.

At the time, this type of training was unheard of, and my running buddies thought I had gone mad. In the early hours of many Saturday mornings I even combined the three disciplines. I biked over the hills to Corsair Bay in Lyttleton Harbour, swam for 30 minutes in the bay, ran for an hour around Lyttleton, and biked home, ready to spend the rest of the day with the family or to catch up on some work.

It occurred to me that combining training sessions gave me an added competitive advantage, since being able to execute one discipline straight after another is the hallmark of triathlon. It was many years later that the Americans 'invented' so-called 'brick training', back-to-back training sessions in different disciplines, specific to triathlon. By then, Erin Baker and I were old hands at it and had refined the method to a degree that is still practised today.

In a New Zealand Herald preview of the 1982 race, the medals had already been decided. Frontrunners were surf lifesaving champion Kim Harker and ex-swimming champion Rick Faulding. Rick had won the previous two years. There was no mention of the sole entry from the South Island. I had no idea what to expect, but the one thing I knew was that I had not travelled that far just to make up the numbers.

The Les Mills New Zealand Ironman Championship event of 1982 consisted of a 1km swim in Mechanics Bay at Teal Park, followed by a 32km out-and-back bike ride along the Auckland foreshore. The 15km run partially retraced the bike course, with the finish in town at the front entrance of the Les Mills Fitness Centre. The run was flat, bar a short steep pinch of an incline to the finish line, up the hill to the gym.

>>>

More than 100 of us lined up for the start, on a wide concrete boat ramp 50m from the water's edge. I was taken by surprise when the gun went off, not used to running starts for swimming events. Once I hit the water, I found myself in a melee of flailing arms and legs. Within no time my goggles were knocked off my head, I was pushed under, swum over and generally swamped.

I got angry. 'You want a fight? Well, you can have it.' I grabbed the person closest to me, got hold of his togs and ripped them clean off his bum. It's an old water polo trick that quickly gets you over and around opponents (and is the main reason why most water polo players wear a double layer of togs). I still wonder today what happened to the poor beggar when he had to exit the water. I delved deeper into my bag of water polo tricks and elbowed and kicked my way out of trouble into semi-clear water. I glimpsed the front swimmers already well ahead. Having lost my goggles I was finding it difficult to see, and I had to rely on the swimmers around me to maintain my direction.

Before I could get into a decent rhythm, the swim exit ramp loomed up. I had decided to keep the first transition simple. In televised reports of the race I'd noticed that most athletes took their time. They had elaborate set-ups with chairs, buckets of water, towels and a complete change of clothing available to them. They also had assistants.

I remained standing, quickly put on my cycling shoes, ran out and hopped on my bike, still in my speedos. I made up valuable time with my novel transition technique and went in chase of the leaders. The big unknown for me was how well they could bike. Drafting was permitted in those early days. Actually, there were few rules and there was no traffic control, bar the odd token marshall, who took his life in his hands when he tried to direct any traffic.

Even then, the Auckland foreshore on a sunny Sunday morning, when church- and beachgoers mingle, resembled the daily traffic jam in the centre of Istanbul. Weaving in and out of the traffic I was abused by irate car drivers, who took fright at this Kamikaze madman dressed only in his speedos, shouting 'Move over!', 'Watch out!' or 'Get out of my way!' in a funny accent. Soon I had the leading bunch in sight. They were to some extent protected by a sole police car, siren on full blast, attempting to free up some road space for them. But this was not France, where motorists are well accustomed to encountering bike races and are quick to retreat to the side of the road to make room for their heroes. I decided to stay with the group. Going up the road on my own seemed too risky as I hardly knew the course, and I didn't want to throw myself back into the chaos of the traffic at the mercy of the ignorant Auckland motoring public.

The safety of being in the group was only relative, as I soon found that none of the other four or five athletes knew how to ride a bike; the safest position was at the front of the bunch. It was a relief to be able to change the bike for my running gear. I had a simple transition strategy, similar to the first one, and I quickly changed my shoewear by using toggles from an old backpack to do up my laces (most still tied their laces the conventional way; elastic laces were still a few years away). I had no socks, chucked on the compulsory competitor's singlet with the race sponsor's name emblazoned on the front, hopped into some running shorts (not wanting to look like an absolute dick – a shirt over speedos was definitely a no-no) and off I went, well before the Aucklanders had settled into their Lazyboys for their rinse, refreshment and change of kit.

I was leading, and by the time I reached the turnaround point there was no one in sight. For the first time in the race I thought: 'I can win this thing.' But you mustn't think that, because as soon as you do something will go wrong, and it nearly did. In my haste and inexperience, I had run the first half as if I was still fresh, ignoring the signs of rapidly accumulating fatigue and the unfamiliar Auckland heat and humidity. I had to slow down. Early shivers warned me of the symptoms of dehydration and heat exhaustion and the last little incline looked and felt like Mt Everest.

Even so, I found myself crossing the finish line with no other competitors close.

This result met with a subdued reception from spectators and media, and murmurs of 'Who the hell is this guy?' rumbled around the hallowed entrance to the Les Mills facility. I had expected to be competitive, but not so convincingly victorious. This, together with my anonymity, made the win extra sweet. An added bonus was that I had finally achieved my boyhood dream of winning an individual national title. It was different from the national title I'd won as part of the New Brighton Harriers road relay team two years earlier, a group of runners already so stacked with talent that I only had to turn up to complete the numbers. It was a special moment that made me want more.

I had no inkling of the journey that this first taste of triathlon success would take me on for the best part of my life.

The difference between me and my competition, I realised, was in my background. I was a mature athlete and I happened to be accomplished in all three disciplines. I was up against some very good athletes, but they were well versed in only one or at the most two sports. They relied on their favoured disciplines to make an impact, but generally struggled through the ones less familiar to them.

I also discovered I was one of the few athletes who'd trained specifically for the event. The others kept doing what they were good at, with a little of the other disciplines thrown in when time permitted. I was well ahead of the game. But that would soon change, as other athletes embraced this exciting new sport to make it their own.

A year after that first victory, I returned to Auckland in 1983 to defend my title and a young upshot by the name of Rick Wells made life difficult for me. Rick had represented New Zealand at the Commonwealth Games in 1982 as a swimmer, and for a while held the national record over-200m freestyle. Cycling professional

Graeme Miller had helped him to improve his bike skills and his very average running form was reconstructed by none other than Allison Roe, winner of the Boston and New York Marathons in 1981. With renowned swimming coach Hilton Brown looking after his swimming, I should have seen it coming. Three coaches against none for me left the odds stacked. I caught all the stronger swimmers on the bike except for Rick, who got off the bike with a healthy lead. I didn't pass him until well into the run for the win.

The following year, 1984, the swim distance was lengthened to 1500m. The bike leg was similar to previous years at 35km, but the course had changed to a circuit that included the notorious Gladstone Road hill. The run was shortened to 12km. I suspected the changes were introduced to give locals, with their swimming prowess, a better chance.

The sea was rough, making the swim even longer than it already was. I left the water two-and-a-half minutes behind Rick, with a few others spread between us. I caught them early on the tough Gladstone Road hill circuit in the expectation of soon seeing Rick ahead of me. But that never happened. Although I made inroads on his lead, it became a long and frustrating chase, and the deficit was still half a minute when I started the run. I didn't panic, as I felt I was the stronger runner.

But I was greedy and set off in pursuit too fast. I caught Rick 3km in, and I tried to drop him there and then so as not to encourage him. But I wasn't feeling so flash and my legs were not responding. My efforts to catch him had caught up with me. Rick ran on my shoulder, with a stoical smile and only a hint of perspiration on his face. He looked comfortable and I felt far from it. We literally slogged it out. He sensed I was struggling, and he put in a burner. Not to be outdone, I had a go as well. It was a display of gamesmanship where neither of us gave an inch. I resigned myself to the fact it was going to come down to a sprint finish.

As in previous years, the finish line was up the short steep hill in front of the main entrance to the Les Mills gym, or at least that's what I thought, and I was confident that I would be able to cover Rick. Even if he looked a tad fresher, there was no way he could match my strength uphill. Although he had slimmed down from his swimming days, he was still a big unit, which would count against him.

The last couple of kilometres felt eternal. Finally, there was the sharp left-hand turn just before the hill and I prepared for one final effort. Out of the corner of my eye I could see Rick ignoring the turn, instead running straight ahead. 'Ah, the stupid bugger is going the wrong way,' I thought, and momentarily I relaxed. At the same time, I looked up expecting to see the finish line. But there was nothing – no banners, no crowd, no noise, just an empty street. It was me who was the stupid bugger. I jogged down and found the finish line on the flat around the next corner, at the back entrance of the facility. The finish line had been changed at the last moment following multiple complaints from the locals that the uphill finish was too tough.

The only one who didn't know was me, the foreigner from the South Island. I have to admit I'd relied on the written course instructions in the race pack, and I hadn't bothered to attend the race briefing where the last-minute change was announced.

I've never missed a race briefing since.

>>>

In the 1980s, the Oamaru Stamina event became a popular South Island triathlon event. It was held in the morning at a time when the region's beloved little blue penguins were already out at sea, oblivious to the action taking place around their breeding grounds.

It was a short-distance event with a quick 400m swim in the harbour, followed by a 30km undulating bike ride around the back roads and a fast 5km run up and down the main street. The whole Oamaru populace was involved with the race one way or another, as participants, volunteers or spectators. The event drew large fields. Although few North Island athletes bothered to come down for it, decent prize money ensured the best of the South were there.

I took part for the first time in 1984. I was confident, since I was in good shape, but as always there were the challengers. One was an ex-semi-professional cyclist whom I had raced against before. He could also run, but the swim generally let him down to the extent that he'd be out of contention by the time he left the water.

I'd built a handy lead after the bike leg, but to my surprise when I ran out of the transition this guy was right on my heels. 'Where the hell did he come from?' I wondered, as I had felt good on the bike and expected him to make little inroad. He looked like the devil possessed. I had a pang of worry. 'Get your shit together, John. Don't let him catch you.' I got to work and he never got close enough, but he had given me a good scare.

After the race, I asked him how he had managed to close the gap. He shrugged his shoulders and said: 'Just had good legs today, mate, that's all.' But stories soon surfaced from other competitors who had seen him come past at 80km/hr holding on to the rear end of a large truck on a long straight bit of road, thereby taking himself from well back in the field to second place. It can be done by skilled cyclists without having to hold on to the truck; just sit in the draft close behind.

It was seen by all those he passed, which was the majority of the field, but protesting was no use. In those days there were few marshals, let alone officials or referees, and nowhere did it say it was illegal. When confronted by angry fellow competitors, he just shrugged his shoulders. If it had not been for the fact the truck had to turn off just before he reached me, he might well have won the race.

In 1984 I competed in a 'quadrathlon' called the Dunedin Fitness Centre Enduro. The race consisted of a swim, bike ride, kayak leg and run, and was held across and around Otago Harbour. At the time, triathlons were not standardised and often included a kayak option. I was confident that as long as the water was flat I would be able to hide my incompetence in that particular discipline and make up for any lost time in my more familiar disciplines. I borrowed a surf ski for the kayak leg. I had never tried one, but judged it a safe bet, since the forecast was for calm weather.

The first discipline, an 800m swim in the harbour, was cold but otherwise uneventful. On the bike, I soon passed the faster swimmers. Leading the race was Dave Gerrard, ex-Commonwealth Games gold medallist in the 200m butterfly and one of the fittest veterans in the country. To get his heavy frames (bike and body) up the steep Dunedin hills, he zig-zagged from one side of the road to the other, a technique that can overcome the severest of gradients but takes more time. I shot straight past him, thinking: 'Mate, if you went up these hills in a straight line you could actually make a good fist of this race.' He was proof that fitness doesn't automatically translate from one discipline to the next.

I arrived at the bike-to-kayak transition with the lead I wanted, but instead of the calm water promised by the weather forecast the previous night, I was met by a sea whipped to a frenzy by an unexpected wind shift. I had no alternative but to jump on the surf ski, bike shoes still on my feet to save time. I capsized instantly into the freezing waters of the harbour. I clambered back on, only to tip out again. I kicked my cycling shoes off, but it made no difference; I kept tipping over as soon as I got back on, pushed over by the waves.

One competitor passed, then another and another. Dave Gerrard was one of them. He gave me an encouraging grin when he came past, just when I had capsized once again. The crowds on the shore were no doubt fascinated by the spectacle unfolding before them. Some shouted well-meant instructions, others just laughed. In a last desperate attempt, I clambered back onto the surf ski but I kept my legs dangling on either side. I stayed upright long enough to start paddling, hesitantly at first but then more firmly.

Anger finally took over and I worked my way across the harbour fuelled by a white hot rage. I remained in the straddled position for the whole journey, as if I was riding a horse. When I got to the other side, I forced my frozen feet into running shoes and went in pursuit of the athletes in front of me. Fed by the recent embarrassment my anger had not waned and I overhauled them all, the last one not far from the finish line. I had the last laugh, but it had been a close call.

Another event with a difference that same year was a run up the 12km-long access road of Mount Hutt, followed by a ride on the ski lift to the top of the mountain and a set course down to the finish at the bottom of the ski slopes. I needed a big lead before the ski section because many ski pros had come out for that race.

My mate Neil Pasco had checked the ski course for me while I ran up the mountain, and was waiting for me at the transition. He went up the lift with me and pointed out the course, marked by flags and set in the shape of a giant slalom on the steepest section of the mountain. It had been raining rather than snowing overnight and the slopes were glistening with ice. 'Bloody heck, Neil. I don't like the look of that.'

Neil told me not to worry as he would be leading. I just had to follow. He was a gun skier, so I was happy with that plan. Following someone is so much easier than finding your own way down a ski slope. But Neil fell on the ice at the first turn and slithered down the mountain, off the course and out of sight. I managed to scrape my way down without mishap, but by the time I hit the finish line my quad muscles were quivering to the point they were ready to snap in half. It was just in time, as the pro skiers were closing in, bombing it down the slope.

Triathlon was taking off not only in New Zealand but worldwide. I was now in my thirties and had difficulty juggling events with my young family, busy general practice and taking papers at Otago University towards a postgraduate diploma in sports medicine, but winning was addictive and so I lurched from one race to the next. I took more and more time off work to train and travel. Invitations to compete nationally and internationally came in. The prize money earned from racing barely covered the cost. I acquired sponsors, like Adidas and Cannondale and the freight company TNT. I disliked approaching possible sponsors, but it had to be done if I was going to continue.

One day, buoyed by successive victories, I called a potential sponsor, who asked me what I did for a job. 'I'm a doctor,' I said innocently. This met with absolute silence. Then came the retort: 'You should bloody well sponsor me!' and the line went dead.

In 1985 I spent time in Australia, America and Europe to compete, but I was not as successful as I'd hoped to be. An obvious choice was a big-money race in Australia with a spectacular course, starting at the Sydney Opera House and finishing in the Royal Botanic Gardens. But the race was a disaster. For the swim across the harbour, the organisers had been given 15 minutes by the harbour authorities to get us across the 800m stretch. They couldn't stop the commercial boat traffic any longer than that, and a boat with a large scoop on the front literally picked up all the stragglers and deposited them ashore at the same time as I clambered out near the front of the field.

The first few cyclists were accompanied by a police car, but the rest of us were not. Only 12 of the 40 traffic lights we encountered were manned. It was mayhem, with plenty of accidents and near misses. The run was equally shambolic. Early on, I passed a truck that was still unloading the first drink station. We had not been briefed about the exact run course: 'It will be clearly marked,' we were told. I was running by myself with no other competitors in sight. At every intersection I took a guess as to which way to go, which is unsettling when you're running at full speed. I got lost towards the end, and crossed the finish line in the opposite direction from that planned. I was furious, and pushed the race director aside when, pretending nothing had happened, he extended his hand to welcome me home.

My official result, 5th, was upheld, and no one was disqualified. The race was followed by the announcement that due to its success it would be even bigger and better the next year, but it didn't happen again for 15 years, when it was the 2000 World Cup event held in preparation for the Olympics later that year.

I tried my luck on the American circuit in 1985 and decided to bring my family. By then we had two daughters, Fleur and Saar, aged five and two. Travelling with a young family in a campervan from race to race was not the best way to prepare for America's highly competitive professional triathlon circuit. My best result was a 4th at one of the longest-surviving events in the world, the Wildflower Triathlon, staged around Lake San Antonio in central California.

Top 10 results were not sufficient to pay the bills. A similar fate befell me in Europe, where I struggled to find form. The whole experience was a reality check that I didn't want to acknowledge. 'Ability delusion' is not an uncommon affliction in our society; it's particularly prevalent amongst the male fraternity, and not limited to sport. Common sense soon took over and I decided to focus on assisting Erin Baker with preparations for her international race debut at the European Ironman Championships, covered in the first chapter.

City of Auckland Triathlon, 1986

On my return from Europe I gradually returned to training. I couldn't stay away from competition for long, and to rekindle my career I targeted the 1986 national championships race. The event was held in Auckland and was now called the City of Auckland Triathlon. (Les Mills had worked out that triathletes were no gym bunnies; the gym giant had achieved its goal of name recognition and pulled out as naming-rights sponsor.) The 1986 event was the first one officially sanctioned by the New Zealand Triathlon Association, established in September 1984. Distances were adjusted to the internationally accepted 1500m swim, 40km bike ride and 10km run, which later became the official Olympic triathlon distances.

I sensed this inaugural sanctioned event was going to be the start of a new, more formal era for our sport and I didn't want to be a spectator. This was a race I really wanted. I knew I was running out of time because of my age and the fact that younger opponents were rapidly closing the gap on me.

Old rival Brett Marshall, a dentist from Matamata, was one of those. He was another super-duper swimmer/surf lifesaver like Rick Wells who had taken to triathlon. For a long time, he had been no threat. Although he swam like a fish, he biked like a kitten and ran like a turtle. He didn't progress as spectacularly fast as Rick in his weak disciplines, although every race it took me a bit longer to catch him.

He had also set his sights on this race and had specifically trained for it. I knew I would be in trouble if we came off the bike together, as I had not run for two months due to a searing pain deep within my right buttock every time I put my foot down. Initially, I thought it was a minor muscle strain, but it hadn't gone away.

Before I knew it, the race was there. Not knowing if I was going to be able to complete the run, I had a doctor friend give me a cortisone injection in the affected area the night before the race. The warm-up jog the next morning did not bode well; the only good thing was that my competition didn't know about my predicament.

I lost my customary two minutes in the swim to Brett and set out in pursuit on the bike. The race was on Auckland's North Shore. The rolling hills of Auckland are very different from the steep and long climbs of the Port Hills in Christchurch. I tried to settle into a rhythm but never felt comfortable. It was not until halfway through the ride that I spotted the flashing lights of the lead car, closely followed by a cyclist, in the distance. It took me another 10km to reach Brett.

It helps when you're in the lead. Invariably you get some unintended assistance from being close behind the lead car or motorbike. I accelerated and swept past Brett, taking over his lead. He dropped back a fraction, enough for me to create a gap and leave him behind. I was desperate to extend my lead so I had a cushion going into the run.

As soon as I ran out onto the course, the pain in my backside came on with a vengeance. I swore and slowed down, ready to pull the pin, but the pain subsided somewhat and I started jogging again. I looked back, could see Brett looming in the distance, so started running a bit faster. By keeping my stride short and the pressure on the affected side to a minimum, I was better able to control the pain. Every now and then, after turning a corner so Brett could not see it, I slowed down to a walk – oh, the relief.

The finish line was looming in the distance. I looked over my shoulder one last time to see that Glenn Davies had overtaken Brett and was closing in fast. But he was too late; I was safe. Relieved, I limped towards the finish line, glad it was over. I was welcomed by a festival atmosphere and a loud: 'There he is, ladies and gentleman, our first official New Zealand triathlon champion. Please welcome the old fox, John Hellemans.'

Ken Henderson was not only the race director, but also the race commentator. I grinned through the pain. 'The old fox – ha, I can live with that.' It was true that at 33 I was much older than most of my opponents and it was also true that I had achieved this victory by foxing the opposition into thinking I was in my usual competitive shape.

Much to my dismay, Mark Watson – another triathlon race commentator who later graduated to the big stage of radio sports commentating in New Zealand – changed 'the old fox' to 'the grey fox', but later, in my Dunedin years, the athletes I coached changed it respectfully to silver fox, which it has been ever since.

The National Triathlon Series comes to Christchurch, 1988

It was rare, and still is, in New Zealand for North Islanders to come south to race. But the lucrative, brewery-sponsored national series held in the late 1980s always included one South Island event, held in Christchurch, forcing the top echelon of North Island triathletes to travel down if they wanted to compete for overall series honours.

The course was brutal. The 1500m swim was held in unpredictable open seas at the Scarborough foreshore in the seaside suburb of Sumner. If the open sea didn't distinguish the men from the boys, the 40-or-so-kilometre bike course definitely would. The first 15 flat kilometres of cycling were pleasant enough, we were usually pushed along by a prevailing easterly tailwind. But then the fun started, with a gut-busting 4km climb up Dyers Pass Road to the Sign of the Kiwi, followed by unrelenting undulations into headwinds on the return journey along Summit Road.

The final 6km down Evans Pass gave the legs some much-needed respite, but you needed the nerves and skills of a rally driver to safely navigate the many bends and turns in the road while descending at an average 70km/hr. The 10km out-and-back run along the water's edge of the Avon-Heathcote Estuary was comparatively sedate, but by then most of the damage had been done.

In early February 1988, Rick Wells came to Christchurch for the first race in the Kiwi Lager Triathlon Series. Rick was vulnerable when not fully fit. I had worked out that the combination of a tough course and a weakened opponent would enhance my chances of success. Rick was known to have a fondness for the sponsor's product and I asked a mate to take him into town for a drink the night before the race.

I looked out eagerly for Rick when I arrived at the race site early the next morning. He wasn't there yet ... good. I paid meticulous attention to the set-up in the transition so I wouldn't lose any valuable time in the change from the swim to the bike. Regardless of his condition I knew I would trail Rick by a considerable margin out of the swim. Meanwhile, there was still no sign of him and I started to get worried he wouldn't show up. That had not been my intention.

Just when the loudspeaker announced it was time for all competitors to clear the transition area, Rick turned up, bleary-eyed. My heart jumped; everything was still going according to plan. From the corner of my eye I saw him hurry through his preparations, urged on by officials. He made the start line only just in time.

My 90-second deficit out of the swim told me all was not well with Rick. Confidently, I started the chase. I planned to pass him on the Dyers Pass Road climb and to do so with such ferocity he would give up there and then. Rick was not the greatest climber and would be unlikely to hang on for long. But just when I got ready to make the sharp left-hand turn indicating the start of the climb, who should be standing on the side of the road with a big grin on his face, pointing at his dead-flat rear tyre. 'You bastard,' I cried out, realising Rick had the last laugh. I won the race, but not in the way I had planned and Rick knew it. My victory that day felt hollow.

Triathlon goes indoors

The weirdest race I have ever taken part in was an indoor triathlon held in Amsterdam. The race was held in 1988 at the RAI Exhibition Centre and it was part of Europe's largest bike expo. I learned about it on the journey to Holland to say goodbye to my terminally ill grandmother. Ien and I had decided to assist her with moving to my parents' house, where she was going to spend her final days.

On the long flight over, after I had exhausted the movies and was unable to concentrate on my book any longer, I pulled the KLM inflight magazine from the seat pocket. A column promoting upcoming shows and events in Amsterdam captured my attention. I jolted awake when I read that the inaugural European Indoor Triathlon Championships would be held as part of Europe's largest bike expo. More than 200 athletes had registered for the event and it was sold out; there was no more information than that. It was February, the height of the triathlon season in New Zealand, so my immediate thought was: I am fit, while the Europeans are only just coming out of winter hibernation.

On arrival, I called Peter Zijerveld, once a European half-ironman champion, who had recently stayed with us in New Zealand for a training camp. It turned out he was an adviser for the event and he got me a start.

I was taken aback, however, when I found out what was involved. At one of the large expo halls, a stage was set up with four stationary bikes, four treadmills and a small pool that just fitted four swimmers side by side. All week, series of four athletes competed against each other over a furious 10 minutes per discipline, with a three-minute transition between each.

The swim was done on a stationary line, attached to a device bolted to the side of the pool that measured your average pulling power. The stationary bike also recorded power output, while the treadmill measured the distance covered over the 10 minutes. A complex mathematical calculation decided which eight athletes would qualify for the two finals held on the last day of the expo.

I borrowed, begged and stole some gear from different stands at the expo and lined up for my turn halfway through the week. By that stage, public interest was picking up and expo visitors together with the triathlon fraternity were following the proceedings in increasing numbers. Large screens and scoreboards kept them informed.

It's really not much fun to swim on a fixed line. The stationary bike I was familiar with, but not the treadmill. After some initial wobbles that cost me valuable time, I soon got the hang of it, and I qualified second fastest for the final.

The atmosphere for the two finals was festive. The exhibitors closed their stalls and celebrated a productive week of trade with plenty of food and drink in the large hall where the final was held. The air was filled not only with loud music, but also with a thick haze of cigarette smoke, as was still common at the time. An announcer kept spectators entertained with introductory chatter. The plate final contested by the four slowest qualifiers went without incident. Spectators picked a favourite and accompanied the spectacle on the stage with loud cheering, jeering and booing. The jeering and booing happened if athletes slowed down at all, which was brutally exposed by the numbers displayed on large scoreboards around the hall.

When it was my turn for the final, the general mood was at boiling point, and the racket similar to what you'd hear in soccer stadiums at weekends all over Holland. During the introductions, through the thick haze, I suddenly caught a glimpse of my father, standing a few rows back from the stage. He had come down with a friend to see what this triathlon thing was all about. He had a bottle of wine in one hand, a half-empty glass in the other and a bewildered look on his face.

The gun went off and we set to work. After the swim, I glanced up at the scoreboard and saw that I was leading by a slim margin. If the others were going to catch me, it would have to be on the bike. European triathletes are usually formidable cyclists and I expected fireworks, but the only commotion came from the back of the hall, where police had to remove some troublemakers from the crowd.

I came off the bike coughing and spluttering from smoke inhalation, but my opponents were no better off. My lead was still intact; in fact, I had extended it a smidgeon. The only uncertainty left was my unfamiliarity with the treadmill. Starting slowly to find my rhythm would cost valuable time, while starting too fast could see me unceremoniously catapulted off the back of the machine.

I started out at a firm 18km/hr and soon found my legs, winding it slowly up to 19.5km/hr, encouraged by loud cheering from the public every time I turned the treadmill up a notch. Buoyed by the crowd, I was running significantly faster than I had done earlier in the week. I was determined not to slow down and suffer the humiliating booing that befell my colleagues when they were forced to turn the speed dial down a fraction.

With the 'finish line' in sight, I cranked the treadmill up to well over 20km/hr for the final sprint home, much to the delight of the fans. It was an unnecessarily risky move, and I nearly paid the price when my legs could not turn over fast enough and my flailing arms couldn't safely reach the speed dial. I was out of control, but just when the treadmill was getting the better of me the siren signalled the end of the race. An official had the presence of mind to hit my treadmill's emergency stop button to save me from becoming a 'most embarrassing moments' phenomenon.

The trophy for coming first was a clock mounted on a mirror, and a beautiful bunch of flowers (the Dutch do flowers well). They went to my grandma later that day. I can still see the hint of a smile that appeared on her haggard face when I carefully placed them next to her on the bedside table.

The birth of the International Triathlon Union

The International Triathlon Union was established in 1989, but the formation of the world body had been preceded by an ugly power struggle. On one side was the well-organised European Triathlon Union, established in 1984 and headed by shrewd Dutch businessman Joop van Zanten. On the other was a poorly organised rest-of-the-world, led by the charismatic Les McDonald. Les was from an English coalmining family and had migrated to Canada, where he became a force in the union movement before seeking a career in sports administration. He had an astonishing record as an athlete, having won his 50-plus age group division at the Hawaii Ironman no fewer than five consecutive times, between 1983 and 1987. Only really tough bastards can do that.

As well as a proven track record in toughness, Les had an uncanny ability to cajole people into doing whatever he wanted, and what he wanted was to be the first president of the International Triathlon Union (ITU). Even van Zanten was no match for Les McDonald.

I was on Joop's side. He was capable, intelligent and honest, spoke at least five languages fluently and had his own ironman successes. He had also made it possible for Erin Baker to compete in the 1985 European Ironman Championships. I urged the

New Zealand Triathlon Association representatives to back the European campaign towards establishing a united global triathlon organisation, but they were already in favour of Les McDonald. Perhaps it was just as well, because if it hadn't been for skilful political manoeuvring by Les and the work done behind the scenes by his side-kick, Loreen Barnett, I'm not sure whether triathlon would have become an Olympic sport.[1]

The first official ITU-sanctioned world championship was held over the Olympic distance in 1989 in Avignon, France. Mark Allen and Erin Baker were the winners. Rick Wells, who had won the unofficial world championship two years earlier in Freemantle, Australia, claimed the bronze medal. I was unable to compete – too many distractions, like paying the bills.

Triathlon makes its debut at the 1990 Auckland Commonwealth Games

Until the instigation of an official world championship, it was not always guaranteed that the best of the world's athletes would show up to championship events. In 1988 at the peak of the stand-off between the European Triathlon Union and Les McDonald, I competed in the self-proclaimed 'world championships' in Kelowna, Canada. McDonald had been responsible for getting the event held in Canada. The Europeans boycotted the race, but omitted to put on a rival event. At that time world triathlon was dominated by Australians and Americans, and Europeans did not play a significant role, apart from Rob Barel from Holland and the Brit, Glenn Cook.

After solid preparation, I ended up 8th in a stacked professional field. To top off a good weekend for New Zealand, Erin Baker won the women's race and Cameron Brown and Sarah Harrow claimed silver in the junior division. Back in New Zealand I was lauded for being the only amateur in a strong field of professional athletes. I begrudgingly had to accept this was true, since I was far more an amateur than a professional. It made me realise that it was unlikely I could compete at that level for much longer.

However, triathlon made its debut at the Commonwealth Games in Auckland in January 1990, a good reason for me to want to extend my career for a bit. The event – despite its status as 'only a demonstration sport' – was the success story of the Games. Auckland showed itself at its best, with blue skies and warm temperatures. There were no other events on that particular day to compete for spectator numbers, and the locals came to the waterfront en masse to watch the spectacle. Crowds were 10 rows deep at some parts of the course. The high spectator numbers paved the way for Olympic inclusion 10 years later.

There was a festive atmosphere, even more so when Erin Baker and Rick Wells won gold medals for their home country. Everyone was celebrating – bar me. I had struggled around the course, anonymously, well back from the action.

It had started so well. I'd trained hard over the winter and was in superb form four months prior to the Games, ready to tackle the qualifying races. We were assigned a full quota of six spots for New Zealand, so I considered the qualifying events a mere formality. Then I got a sore throat. 'No worries – a few easy days and I'll be fine,' I thought.

But the sore throat didn't go away, and after a couple of weeks of taking it easy I was starting to lose some of my hard-won fitness. I went back to training and ignored the symptoms. It didn't go well: my times were slower and I didn't feel good. Even so, I trained harder than ever and had dug myself into a deep hole by the time the first selection event was held in Auckland in early November, three months before the Games.

I finished 5th, my place in the team suddenly under threat, with the second selection race coming up one month later. With foolish determination I kept ignoring the signals from my body. Somehow I surpassed myself at the second selection race, finishing a distant 2nd behind Rick.

Rick led the team, which also included the in-form Bruce Baxter, Roger Clark (now the CEO of my favourite rugby team, the Dunedin-based Highlanders) and two young bolters, Dunedin PE student Ian Edmond, and John Hughes, a cyclist-turned-triathlete I was coaching.

The Games were coming closer and there were no signs of improvement. I needed a miracle to turn things around. But, as I've always said, miracles only happen to the religious and the gullible, so I kept training and arrived at the race fooling myself that things were not too bad and all I needed was a good day.

After a choppy swim, I was well out of contention, two minutes down on the lead group. Where I would normally make some gains on the bike, I now had difficulty holding my own. The bike course took in my favourite Gladstone Road hill climb but this time it felt like a mountain, my heavy legs turning round in what felt like slow motion. The run was no better. I felt awful and was happy to see the finish-line. 'End of career,' was my first thought. The second was: 'Not a nice way to go'.

Equipment revolution

I took a break and in time recovered both my health and my spirits. Before long I was planning a comeback. In my desire to keep up with the competition I became obsessed with any improvements I could make to my equipment, in particular in relation to cycling. Aerodynamics was all the rage, a trend started off in 1984 by the Italian cyclist Francesco Moser. He was the first to use an aerodynamically designed bike, which featured a smaller-sized front wheel, steel aerofoil tubing, bullhorn handlebars and closed-in wheels, front and rear.

He used it in his attempt to beat the one-hour record of 49.431km set 12 years earlier by the best cyclist of all time, Belgian Eddie 'The Cannibal' Merckx. Moser also wore the first skinsuit in further aid of aerodynamics. He smashed the record at 50.808km. Four days later he extended it to 51.151km. It was suspected later that he had also used blood-doping, which was not illegal at the time.[2]

Low-profile bikes – aptly referred to as 'funny bikes' – were embraced by triathletes in the late 1980s. Bauer, my bike sponsor at the time, had one custom-built for me according to my specifications. The bike had a normal 27-inch rear wheel, but there any comparison with a conventional bike stopped. It had a down-sloping top tube to accommodate the smaller 26-inch front wheel, combined with a forward-sitting seat post – courtesy of the same aircraft engineer who had constructed my first set of aerobars, and as solidly built, so it wouldn't snap. This resulted in a body position so far forward and downwards my nose just about touched the front wheel.

The problem with my super-aerodynamic position was that the only thing I could see was the ground underneath the bike. As soon as I lifted my head, I felt a searing pain in my neck and shoulders. I called it 'aero neck' and later published my findings in a medical journal, becoming the first to introduce this brand new clinical condition to the medical world.

I explored solutions for a cure. I knew that other athletes solved the problem with a complex set-up of mirrors attached to their helmet and bike. I found my answer in a Dutch triathlon magazine, in an article on the ingenious invention of 'prism-glasses', which allowed you to see in front of you while looking down (if that makes sense).

I had to have a pair, but time was of the essence. As luck would have it, I knew the inventor, Goof Schep, an amicable Dutch sports doctor who would have made a seriously good triathlete if he had been able to swim. Many years before, when I was still a student, we had both competed at the World Medical Games. I called Goof and he sent me a prototype by express mail, smelling a lucrative export market Down Under. I was excited when the glasses arrived, and put them straight to the test.

The contraption sits on your face like a pair of reading glasses, but couldn't look more different. The thick lens sticks out from your face in an unnatural horizontal fashion. Somehow, when you look down at the thick prisma glass it catches the scene in front of the bike and transfers it mysteriously to the back of your eyeballs. At least, that was the idea. The glasses – complemented by my recently obtained aero-helmet, a hand-me-down from world duathlon champion and aero-freak Matt Brick – made me look like an alien. I didn't care. Dressed in full combat gear I took to the streets of Christchurch with my newly acquired weapons.

With a few mighty pedal strokes on my bike I got up to speed, head down in the aero-position. And saw exactly nothing. Within no time, I rode smack-bang into the rear of a parked car. Bewildered passers-by scraped me and my bike off the back of the car and, having ascertained that I was unhurt, left me to it, their looks suggesting they weren't sure whether I was more deserving of contempt or pity.

Giving up on the glasses, I returned to adjusting the bike. By using numerous washers to raise the handle bars to be more upright, I found a position in which my neck was not so strained when looking up. This took the 'low' well and truly out of the 'low-profile' bike, eradicating any aerodynamic advantage. At least I still maintained the psychological advantage, I told myself, as the bike still looked pretty mean. Suffice to say, the prism-glasses never became a commercial success.[3]

Around the time that the low-profile bike became fashionable, the seat shifter came into being. The forward-angled seat post was an advantage on the flat when biking in full aero position, elbows resting on the handlebars. But when you're climbing, the aero position doesn't work and is not needed anyway, as the speed is reduced to the extent that frontal resistance matters less. It also helps when climbing if you can pull up on the handle bars while pushing down with your legs, transferring extra power onto the pedals, using a technique that goes by the exotic name of 'honking'.

Sitting upright on a bike with a forward seat position doesn't feel right and results in sub-optimal power transfer to the pedals on the uphill, and far too much weight on the front wheel when descending. The seat shifter was just the solution to this problem. With a quick pull on a small lever on the handlebars, you pushed your seat to a forward (for the flat) or backward (for the hills) position. It sounded as simple and ingenious as the aerobar.

The first time I tried it in a local time-trial competition, I pulled the lever and shoved my behind hard backwards just before I hit an incline in the road. Nothing happened. I doubled my effort with the next try and this time the seat shot backwards, straight off the rails, with me still attached to it. With my feet clipped firmly into my pedals, my backside had nowhere to go but onto the rear wheel. It stopped me and my bike dead in our tracks. I toppled over into the ditch on the side of the road, feet still locked into the pedals and bum to the rear wheel. It hurt, and I would have cried out in agony if I hadn't been so mortified. Instead, I unclicked my pedals and quickly got up before anyone could see me.

'You okay?' a passing competitor yelled politely, clearly with no intention of stopping for anything. I nodded and pretended I was tightening the seat bolt on my bike. But the seat, shifter included, was broken beyond repair. I left it in the ditch and rode home standing. It was another invention weighing half a ton that never took off.

Dressing up for the World Championships, Orlando, 1990

Having missed the first official world championship event in Avignon, and seeking redemption for my poor performance at the Commonwealth Games, I was hungry for success at the triathlon event in Orlando, Florida, in September 1990. It was also a good opportunity to put my 'funny bike' to the test. I knew the swim-to-bike transition was going to be a crucial part of the race for me because I would be lagging behind out of the water. Aged 37 I could not rely on my biking strength any more to close the gap. Despite the non-drafting rule (7m between bikes, unless passing) the dynamics and size of the groups were such that there was a significant advantage to being with a group compared to riding solo. You can still get a good draft 7m behind another competitor, particularly when you sit further back in a larger group. Besides, the draft busters were generally too lenient. Rather than penalising half the field, they would prefer to avoid penalising anyone or to make only the odd example.

Another new rule had come into play. Most triathlons around the world were held on Sunday mornings. Unsuspecting church-goers were not only confronted with traffic jams caused by triathlon races, but also by cyclists and runners dressed only in speedos and, in the case of the women, skimpy togs. That sight was too much for some, and race organisers received a raft of complaints about 'indecent exposure'.

The ITU took the lead and banned bare chests. We were instructed that torsos must be covered at all times during the bike ride and run. Consequently in the swim-to-bike transition we faced a mighty challenge to ensure we were half decent. Singlets were most popular because they were easiest to put on. The usual technique was to throw it around your neck, hop on your bike, and work your torso into the singlet while already on the move. Comic situations arose when riders put their arms or head through the wrong holes of their singlet, getting their arms caught behind their back or their head stuck and nearly strangling themselves in the process. Crashes caused by these 'wardrobe malfunctions' were not uncommon, and at best they cost athletes valuable time.

Then, eureka, a few days before the Orlando race I found the answer. I asked Erin Baker if I could borrow one of her New Zealand team swimsuits for the race. Initially, she thought I was joking, but she soon realised I was serious. She handed me a swimsuit on the condition that I would not return it.

Needless to say, there was the issue of size. How do you get a large male body (184cm tall) into an extra-small woman's swimsuit? Indeed, with difficulty. But with some stretching and tearing of the fabric and rearranging of certain body parts, I was able to squeeze into the suit. I was worried others would copy me, which would put paid to my advantage. But at the practice swim the day before the race I was ridiculed and laughed at to such an extent by my teammates, there was no risk of them following my example.

'I'll have the last laugh,' I figured. When I came out of the water, I saw the first bunch of athletes in transition busy covering their torsos with varying degrees of success, leaving the transition in a long line with many still re-arranging their fabric. The only thing I had to do was hop on my bike and go in pursuit. Just when the loose bunch had started to get organised, I arrived at the tail end and went along for the ride for the remainder of the bike leg.

Two athletes were up the road from our large bunch of about 12 – Rick Wells and Mike Pigg. They had formidable rides, which kept them ahead of our group, but they paid the price on the run. It was my first experience with group riding and I couldn't believe how easy it was. No wonder I hadn't been able to bridge any gaps after the swim lately.

Other athletes in the group looked at me strangely in my swimsuit and one asked if I was sure I was in the right race. What I hadn't counted on was the heat and humidity once our feet hit the tarmac for the run. Training through the Christchurch winter had not prepared me for temperatures well above 35°C and humidity peaking at 86% during the run. Soon I was in trouble.

The brain said no, while the body wanted to push on. We have an inbuilt defence mechanism that kicks in on such occasions – the body goes automatically into survival mode. When it is depleted of energy or just exhausted or, in this case, overheated, it can't overrule the brain, which is busy giving signals to the muscles to slow down in order to prevent a total meltdown. Scientists call this the 'central governor'. In this state, the only thing you can do is work with whatever the brain allows you to do and get to the finish as best you can.

Drifting back through the field, I started to feel self-conscious about my appearance for the first time. I wished I could hide. The backdrop for the run didn't help: it wound through the Disney theme park. Most visitors to the park had never seen a triathlon and the race was not the reason they had come. They looked at us, perplexed, perhaps not sure whether this was all part of the theme park's attractions. I received particularly curious looks, or maybe I was just self-conscious. My swimsuit was so tight the straps had by then burned through the skin onto my collarbones and the chafing in my crotch was unbearable.

These distractions aside, the urge to finish took over. I struggled across the finish line in 33rd position. As it was, many of the New Zealand athletes, and athletes from other countries with temperate climates, had been in a similar predicament to me, including Rick Wells, who had come off the bike with a decent lead but faded to 10th. Erin Baker, like Rick, rode by herself, ahead of a pack containing her main opposition. For her as well, the effort to stay ahead combined with the oppressive heat took too much out of her and she finished just outside the podium in 4th place.

The medical care at the finishing line was a shambles, with a lack of staff, beds and equipment. My medical training as well as instinct took over and I quickly got myself hydrated and went to the aid of my fellow competitors where I could, but not before putting on a tee-shirt and shorts to cover up the forerunner of the modern tri-suit. I should have patented the idea; it would have been worth the embarrassment and pain.

GenkaiTriathlon,1991: Water, water, everywhere ...

In early 1991, together with New Zealand women's triathlon champion Erin Christie, I travelled to Japan at the invitation of the Japanese Triathlon Association to take part in the Genkai Triathlon. Japan is a wonderful place to compete: the races are extremely well-organised and the Japanese treat you like royalty.

The start of the race was on a small beach. I lined up with 500 mainly Japanese athletes and a handful of other overseas competitors, behind a rope that was a mere 10m long. With so many athletes in so little space, I expected the start to bring carnage. To secure my position, I stood hard up against the rope well before the official start time. I was the only one to do so: the Japanese athletes lined up in orderly fashion behind me. There was no cajoling, pushing or elbowing forward. They even respectfully maintained space between each other. In honour of my guest status, they stood back and gave me friendly smiles, all the while bowing their heads with endless repetition, right up until the gun went off. It was rather unsettling.

With the start gun, I was first to enter the water, completely unhampered. The Japanese 1500m freestyle champion slotted in at my feet and stayed there for most of the swim, which I felt took politeness a bit far. The 2km course was set out by a lane rope that was exactly a kilometre long. It reached far into the sea and had a large orange buoy at the end. We swam out on one side and back on the other. Nowhere else in the world could this have worked; the temptation to limit time loss by diving under the rope before the official turnaround would be too great for many. But in Japan cheating results in such loss of face that it is very rare. For that reason, Japan is also probably the only country in the world where the no-drafting rule for the bike works perfectly fine. No draft busters required.

The main obstacle in the water was the thick layer of stinging jellyfish we had to swim through. Within no time my exposed face, hands and feet were burning with pain. Just as well it was a wetsuit swim so the rest of my body was protected.

With the lead group out of the water and after a quick transition, I was first to head out on the bike course. Hydration over the 60km undulating course was crucial because the heat and humidity were already intense, despite the 7am start. Why so many of the big international races are held in hot and humid climates is beyond me.

I had a special contraption mounted under my seat called a 'bike stream'. Launched as the new revolution in hydration a few months earlier, it was a rubber balloon filled with 2 litres of water. A plastic tube inserted into the balloon was guided along the top tube of the bike and re-appeared at the centre of the handle bars. All I had to do was to bend down and put the end of the tube in my mouth, bite on the valve and presto, the contents from the balloon squirted straight into my stomach with such power I didn't even have to swallow. But at the first intersection, disaster struck. I hadn't expected such a large crowd, which was rows deep, everyone waving little flags and cheering politely. Distracted by the sight, I rode my rear wheel into a pothole and at the same time the balloon under my seat exploded in spectacular fashion. I didn't see it, but I certainly felt it.

The spectators did see it. Their faces froze in the most comical expressions, best described as different stages of shock and terror: what the hell had happened right under the Speedos of that tall foreigner on his funny bike? Catastrophe averted, nonetheless alarm bells rang in my mind. How was I going to survive without access to fluids? There were no drink stations on the bike leg and while I knew I would likely get through the ride without fluids, things were bound to get ugly on the run if I came off the bike with a fluid deficit.

I had a two-minute lead after the bike ride. I did not feel well, had the dreaded goosebumps, and my legs responded only sluggishly when I commanded them to switch to run mode. By then it was 38°C and I still had 16km to run. Drink stations were positioned every 2km and they became my targets. There were three different tables at every station, from which volunteers handed out drinks. They called out in Japanese what the drinks were, so that was no help. At the first station, I ended up with a sports drink that came straight back up, as it was far too concentrated. At the second station, an enthusiastic volunteer pushed a cup into my hand crying out, 'Miso!'

'Miso soup, for god's sake,' I thought. 'That's the last thing I want.' But the drink was cold and tasted like water. It turns out that 'mizu' is the Japanese word for water.

From there on I lurched from drink station to drink station, yelling for mizu. The mizu saved me – together with the fact that my pursuers were not in much better shape than me. Delirious, I collapsed over the finish line next to a water trough, from which I drank greedily for the next half an hour, photographed and filmed by an amused Japanese press corps.

The only foreign athlete who didn't look worse for wear was my New Zealand team mate Erin Christie, who won the women's race by 15 minutes. 'I loooove the heat,' she confided later. At the after-race party, the Japanese lost much of their reserve, which made it one to remember.

King of comebacks

I became the king of comebacks. Every time I entered a race I announced it would be my last, as work and family pressures were becoming too much. I meant it every time, but later I would plan my comeback – just one more race. It resulted in me racing every race as if it was to be my last, which it was … until the next one. You don't want your last race to be a failure or even mediocre, so that became the fuel for my motivation and competitiveness.

My friends soon figured me out and would laugh knowingly each time I declared: 'I'm done, this is truly my final race.' (Once I finally realised what was happening, I joked that the only good reason to retire is so you can make a comeback.) It drove Ien to distraction because she takes what people say at face value and that included my retirement announcements. She fell for it every time – but then, so did I.

It became a bone of contention between Ien and me during the later years of my career as an elite triathlete, when she found it difficult to reconcile herself to yet another comeback. One evening when the kids were tucked up in bed, she came looking for me and found me in the spare room on my indoor bike trainer, engrossed in my efforts, the sweat pouring off. The sight made her sink to her knees and sob.

It gave me a fright and I got off my bike to give her a hug. But then I retreated to the shower, session cut short, feeling a slight sense of irritation – a sign of neurotic-obsessive behaviour threatening to break through. Singlemindedness in making training a priority is an admirable and necessary character trait in athletes, but an almost inevitable side effect at some stage is a loss of perspective.

One year, when both daughters were still under the age of five, I went out for an early-morning bike ride on Christmas Day, leaving Ien in charge of the kids and with brunch to prepare. We had friends coming over, but I assured her I would be back well before then. At the furthest point of my three-hour ride, my newly acquired titanium crank snapped in half, causing me momentarily to black out when my crotch landed on the top bar of the bike.

It was 8am. I walked up to the closest farm, still some distance away. The curtains were closed and my knocks on the door went unanswered. The next farm was a good walk away, but more luck this time. I called Ien and asked her if she could pick me up. She bundled the kids in the car and came to get me. Not much was said on the way home and I have never been out training on Christmas Day since.

On another occasion during a rainy family camping holiday in the Marlborough Sounds, I rode my bike on the indoor bike trainer in the tent and swam in the bay, tied to an elastic cord attached to a buoy, neglecting my role as a husband and father. Suffice to say, upon reflection, these are not my proudest moments.

The combined camping and training holiday was in preparation for the 1991 national championships held in Wellington in January. My training paid off. After 30km on the bike I caught a small lead group, of which I considered myself the best runner. I was already preparing my victory speech when I heard the loud bang of a blown tyre.

'Good,' I thought, 'One less competitor to worry about', just as I felt my rear wheel going 'bonkedebonkedebonk'. For once I wasn't carrying a spare, so it was the end of my race. A win would have helped me to rationalise my anti-social behaviour in the weeks leading up to the race, but this setback made me think: perhaps it was meant to give me a message.

My (subconscious) strategy of quitting and coming back had kept the fire going well beyond my use-by date. Despite being in my late 30s, I wasn't going much slower, but the exponential increase in pace and depth of competition meant I had to be 110% prepared for every race, something I hardly ever achieved.

The costs, mentally and financially, had become a burden. In the early days of my career, race invitations, sponsorship and prize money went some way towards justifying my part-time athletic career, but those sources had long since dried up.

Busted

The penultimate straw came at the 1992 world championships in Huntsville, the largest town in the Muskoka region of Ontario, Canada.

I was 39. I was better prepared than ever, courtesy of three weeks of altitude training in Boulder as a guest of Erin Baker and Scott Molina. I felt strong, and after a good swim I ended up in a large lead bunch that included all the favourites. I was in for a good one.

The no-drafting rule still applied and the usual careful juggling for position went on. Our group was accompanied by three motorbikes carrying draft busters on the passenger seats, but although there was blatant drafting going on, they did absolutely nothing. As a consequence, we became more and more careless and ended up riding like the peloton in the Tour de France.

Then the draft buster hit. I can still see him clearly in front of me, a big fat guy with his head buried in a large motorbike helmet. Triumphantly, he pointed a yellow card at me. I processed his action in slow motion. I couldn't believe it, because we were all riding in similar positions in the pack. Either everyone was drafting or nobody was. From the corner of my eye I noticed another rider

ABOVE: With Erin Baker: a successful partnership.

LEFT: Pre-race concentration, 1987 Hawaii Ironman.

BELOW: Swim start, 1987 Hawaii Ironman.

LEFT: Erin competing in the 1987 Hawaii Ironman. (Bob Babitt; photograph by Lois Schwartz)

BELOW: The hat incident, 1987 Hawaii Ironman.

My father and me,
c. 1960.

Three generations:
sandwiched between
my father and my Opa,
c. 1963.

TOP: It all started with a career in swimming and water polo, c. 1972.

BOTTOM: Greet (bow) and Nicolette (stroke), my two younger sisters, won silver in the double sculls at the 1984 Los Angeles Olympic Games. (Harry Meijer)

TOP: Off to New Zealand, 1978.

BOTTOM: An unconventional wedding, Whites Bay, Marlborough Sounds, 1979. (Peter Haeni)

ABOVE: My mother in the 1990s, absorbed in her favourite activity, reading, in her favourite spot at Lake Paterswolde.

LEFT: Graham Smart, medical superintendent at Wairau Hospital from 1950 to 1980. (Dawn Sanders)

BOTTOM LEFT: Roly Crighton, coach for successful athletes including swimmer Sophie Pascoe and triathlete Andrea Hewitt. (High Peformance Sport New Zealand)

BOTTOM RIGHT: Duncan Laing, legendary swimming coach of double Olympic gold medallist Danyon Loader, amongst others. (Laing family collection)

TOP: 1982 Les Mills New Zealand Ironman Championship race: my first triathlon, and my first win.

BOTTOM: A convincing victory and a subdued reception: 1982 Les Mills New Zealand Ironman Champion race.

TOP: Side-by-side with Rick Wells (and closely followed by his supporters), 1984 Les Mills New Zealand Ironman Championship race.

BOTTOM: 1988 World Championships Kelowna Canada. L to R: Glenn Cook (GB), Ken Glah (USA), Mark Allen (USA) and me, mopping my brow. (International Triathlon Union (ITU))

John Hellemans had a good day and
stood out from the rest of the boys in his
Bendon bathers.

TOP: The equipment revolution. My low-profile 'funny
bike': the super-aerodynamic downwards position led to
visibility problems and 'aero neck'.

ABOVE: The ingenious invention of 'prism-glasses', which
were designed to enable you to see in front of you while
looking down.

LEFT: Borrowing Erin's swimsuit: my 'Bendon shocker' at
the 1990 World Championships, Florida. (Arthur Klap, *New
Zealand Triathlete* Issue 32 October 1990)

TOP: Genkai triathlon, 1991: dehydration, cameras and microphones: not a good combination.

BOTTOM: The New Zealand men's triathlon team for the Commonwealth Games, Auckland, 1990; it was the first time that triathlon featured in these games. L to R: Rick Wells, Ian Edmond, me, Roger Clark, Bruce Baxter. (Triathlon NZ)

LEFT: 'Noise': Andrea Hewitt, the most consistent female athlete on the ITU circuit. (ITU)

BELOW: Kitzbühel in 2007: Andrea leaving the water in commanding position; it was to be her first World Cup win. (ITU)

ABOVE: Andrea wins the 2017 Abu Dhabi WTS event in a sprint finish from Jodie Stimpson (GBR). (ITU)

LEFT: Inseparable: Laurent Vidal and Andrea Hewitt. (Jordi Bosc)

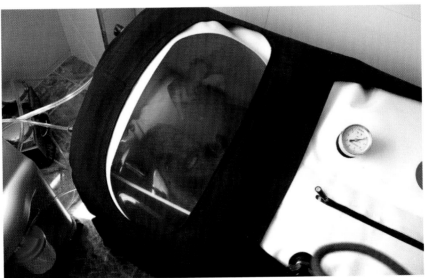

TOP LEFT: 2007 Beijing World Cup: Kris Gemmell finishes in 4th place, qualifying for the 2008 Olympics. (ITU)

TOP RIGHT: Bevan Docherty and Kris Gemmell, mates finishing in 3rd and 4th place respectively in the 2007 Beijing World Cup. (ITU)

BOTTOM: Preparing for the 2008 Beijing Olympics included hyperbaric treatment for Kris's foot injury. Kris 'salutes' me from the safety of the hyperbaric chamber.

TOP: 2008 Kitzbühel World Cup. L to R: Laurent Vidal, Sven Riederer, Kris Gemmell, Ivan Vasiliev and Bevan Docherty chasing the eventual winner Iván Raña who is out of sight. (ITU)

BOTTOM: A Kiwi coaching the Dutch team. Mooloolaba, Australia, 2012. L to R: Rachel Klamer, Neiske Becks, Danne Boterenbrood, Sarissa de Vries and Maaike Caelers. (Adrie Berk)

TOP: The start of the 2013 Hawaii Ironman (bike racks on the pier on the left). (FinisherPix)

BOTTOM: Out in the lava fields, 2013 Hawaii Ironman. (FinisherPix)

TOP: Entering 'death march' territory,
2013 Hawaii Ironman. (FinisherPix)

BOTTOM: The finish line, 2013 Hawaii Ironman. (FinisherPix)

getting the same treatment from the second referee. The calls were completely random.

In that short moment, my world caved in. I stopped, as was the requirement at the time, and watched the bunch disappear into the distance. I had to stand still with my bike lifted off the ground for as long as the referee saw fit. Protesting would only result in prolonging the penalty, so I underwent the humiliation as stoically as I could, furious at the injustice.

For the remainder of the bike leg I was in no-man's-land between two bunches, one too far up the road to catch, the other too far back to wait for. Soon after finishing, still fuming, I managed to make a fool of myself by barging into a referees' meeting, closely followed by an anxious Arthur Klap, our team manager. There I stood, clad in my singlet and skimpy togs, in front of a hostile and silent group of well-dressed officials, sitting around a table sifting through their papers. I demanded rectification of the injustice handed out to me. The head referee, a guy with schnauzer eyebrows perched above piercing small grey eyes, looked up, He listened to my tirade for a short moment before putting his hand up for me to stop.

His eyes narrowed until they all but disappeared under his shaggy brows, his face turned the colour of a ripe tomato, and he seemed about to explode with fury. His voice trembling with the effort to contain himself, he asked me if I had been drafting during the race. I could not blatantly lie and said, 'Yes, but … ' Before I could carry on, his hand went up again to stop me. He then looked down and resumed his paper shuffling, signalling the end of the conversation.

His complexion had quickly returned to a more acceptable shade. For him, my admission had closed the case. As with the law of the land, the rules in sport are not always about fairness.

For some time thereafter, I considered quitting all association with a sport that had rules that were as un-refereeable and ridiculous as the ground-contact rule in racewalking.[4]

But leaving the sport would have been too easy. Instead, I became a firm and outspoken protagonist of drafting. Although I could see the disadvantage of turning an individual race into a group race, this was outweighed by the fact triathlon would once again become a race decided by athletes, rather than by dubious judgement calls from referees. I applauded the ITU when they started to introduce drafting in 1994. It was too late for me, but it saved the sport at elite level and paved the way for Olympic inclusion.

The newly started ITU World Cup series came close to home with an event at the Gold Coast in 1993, and I decided to have one more crack at it. I was now a veteran athlete at 40 and put myself under enormous pressure to get ready. Three or four training sessions a week for each discipline did not cut it any more: longer sessions were required, and more of them.

I promised myself I would retire from elite competition if I didn't make the top 10. In that case, I would either become an age grouper or do something different altogether, like table tennis. I liked table tennis, or at least I liked the idea of it. I came 11th.

Age groupie

I took a break, forgot about table tennis and stuck to what I knew best. I won my first amateur age group world championship triathlon title in 1994 in Wellington, in the 40–45 age group. It was the start of a long amateur career.

The 40–45 group is the most competitive because it's filled with frustrated ex-pros like me, along with super-fit guys who for some reason didn't take the step up to racing professionally before. You can still be really fit at the age of 40. That, combined with the experience of knowing how to dig deep, makes the racing pretty intense. The combination of a more relaxed attitude in training and there being less at stake when racing – but still being able to let the competitive juices run free – worked well for me. I picked my races carefully and avoided flat courses where drafting was rife. Events also had to fit in with my coaching, and sometimes I had to forgo a race for some unplanned coaching duty, but I didn't mind.

Over the years, I won eight amateur age group world titles and came second once. That was in Mexico, a year after my win in Wellington, and it was one of the most memorable events for all the wrong reasons. I went to Mexico a bit undercooked, though confident that I would still be able to be competitive, but thanks to the unrelenting heat and a formidable opponent I ended up cooking my goose instead. Halfway into the bike ride I was in the lead when I heard what sounded like a jet plane coming up behind me. Before I had time to look back it was upon me – and not a jet but a rocket-powered spaceship came roaring past, a bicycle in its most aerodynamic and futuristic form. Stretched out horizontally across its frame was the American Mac Martin, his head hidden within an enormous helmet, no doubt intended to complement the wind-cheating characteristics of the bike. The noise, a deep disconcerting rumble, came from its rear wheel which was completely enclosed, creating psychedelic white patterns as it turned. 'Shit,' I thought 'here's trouble ...' and accelerated with one mighty heave so that I could slot in behind the rocket ship.

The draft legal distance was still seven metres, but I had difficulty staying there so I inched a bit closer. The American did not like that one bit and immediately started to make life difficult for me. He would slow down then suddenly jump away, accelerating with such force that by the time I caught up with him again I was seeing stars. I knew I could not keep this up for long if I wanted to survive the run. In fact, I should have just let him go and rely on being able to catch him up after the bike ride. Surely the American, who had thighs the size of my waist, wouldn't cut it on the run? Suddenly he changed tactics and started weaving across the road, from right to left and left to right, looking back and abusing me, 'You drafting bastard, get off my fucking wheel!' It was most annoying, even if he was right about the drafting, but it took the fun out of the cat-and-mouse game so I let him go with 10km of the ride still to cover. 'See you on the run, buddy,' I thought, still optimistic.

As soon as I started the run, I was hit by the suffocating 40 degrees temperature and 80% humidity, and my legs were cooked from the ride; whatever I tried I could not get them going. I knew I had to start looking after myself if I wanted to make the finish line, so it became a race of survival, from drink station to drink station, just putting one leg in front of the other. I was sure someone would catch me but I didn't care. Let me finish, I thought desperately, just let me finish. And I did, but only just. The finishing area was chaos, littered with the prostrate bodies of age groupers who had started ahead of us, some writhing in agony, others not moving, just lying there. There was no medic or paramedic in sight. I removed myself from the area with my last drop of energy, not in a condition to help any of them, and collapsed under a palm tree where I stayed, drifting in and out of consciousness, for the next couple of hours.

I was finally found by a mate who carried me to my hotel, not too far from the race.

My best age-group victory of all was in 2003, when the world championships were held in in Queenstown, where I raced in the 50–54 category. The pristine lake and rolling terrain surrounded by white-topped mountains provided an inspiring background. My workmates had come out to cheer me on, and I was in good shape. We had to run six laps on an undulating golf course circuit and I managed to lap all competitors in my age group, to finish 10 minutes ahead of second.

CHAPTER 5
THE COACH

After Erin Baker

At the height of Erin Baker's reign, in the late 1980s, I was approached by other athletes for coaching support. As Erin's adviser, I got a lot of credit for her winning ways, although in all honesty she was the kind of athlete who would have done just as well if she had been coached by a doorknob. But I was vain enough to enjoy my new-found fame as a coach and I liked the idea of turning a few more lemons into world champions. It sounded easy enough, but I soon discovered that it wasn't, and that not all athletes were like Erin Baker. Some would not respond to my training methods or could not cope with my direct (some call it confrontational) coaching style; others would get injured or sick. None was as tough as Erin, the benchmark I measured them against.

I set to work, aided by the coach support programmes offered by the New Zealand Sports Foundation, which today is called High Performance Sport New Zealand. I attended coaching conferences, listened to more experienced coaches and learned about sport science, what it can do and, more importantly, what it can't.

The networking with coaches from other sporting codes was invaluable. I visited training sessions, games and competitions and observed how they went about their business. I learned that all athletes have not only their own personality, but also their own unique physiology. To get the most out of the athletes I had to respect that and work with whatever it was that made the athlete tick.

In team sports, the team comes before the individual athlete. This does not apply to sports like triathlon, where the individual has to come first. This is the main reason why it is difficult to create a robust team culture for national, regional and professional triathlon teams.

>>>

From the late 1980s, I coached a number of promising female athletes. One was Jenny Rose, a Canterbury rugby representative vying for selection to the Black Ferns, who were just as dominant on the world scene as their male counterparts, the All Blacks. Her rugby team entered a triathlon as part of pre-season conditioning and Jenny not only won it, but liked it.

Jenny has a bubbly and sociable personality and she wanted to have fun. She wanted to participate in both rugby and triathlon, but I told her the combination of rugby, triathlon and fun was not going to work if she wanted to take either sport seriously and that she had to make a choice. She chose triathlon ... and fun. Initially, it was not always easy to keep her on task, as her active social life would often get in the way of her main aim of developing good training habits. She had lost the little finger of her right hand in a farming accident as a youngster and this was a real disadvantage in the swim. She never complained about it, though, and when I suggested she get a prosthesis she just laughed.

At her first big national event, held in Wellington, Jenny jumped on her bike a bit too enthusiastically, crashed and cut the bottom of her foot open on her front chain ring. It was a nasty cut and she was unable to continue. She was devastated and in a lot of pain. I went with her to hospital and, not sure how to console her, told her that this experience would make her stronger. She told me later that my words made a deep impression on her and motivated her to strive for greater success.

I've learned that as a coach your words can have a powerful effect, but not always as intended. A spontaneous remark like that, offered as words of comfort, can have a big impact on an athlete's career, while a carefully thought-out sermon can go in one ear and out the other. You never really know which until the athlete tells you later.

Jenny was the ITU World Triathlon Series champion in 1994, and she won the World Long Distance Triathlon Championships in Nice a year later, stepping in Erin Baker's footsteps. Early in 1996, she finished 2nd in the New Zealand Ironman.

At the Nice triathlon a few months later, she was looking to repeat her win from the previous year. On the bike she was just about to pass Sophie Delemere from France on a steep downhill section, when Sophie crashed. In an attempt to avoid her, Jenny crashed head-first into a stone wall. It knocked her out cold. She suffered post-concussion fatigue for a long time and struggled to make a full recovery.

At the ITU world champs in Perth in 1997 Jenny looked to be back in some sort of shape, but she lost a bike shoe in an uncharacteristically clumsy move in the swim-to-bike transition, and lost contact with the first bunch. Her race was over. I was furious and told her so as soon as she had finished. 'Jenny, that was pathetic,' I said. I should have known to wait and reserve my feedback until later, when emotions had settled. She took exception to my outburst and changed to another coach.

Jenny is now a successful triathlon coach herself, based in Wellington. Fortunately, she's not one to hold a grudge for long and we get along well.

Sarah Harrow was 18 and a successful age-group swimmer when we met. Her dad, a champion swimmer and surf lifesaver, had taken to triathlon and inspired her to try her hand at the new sport. Sarah was mentally and physically tough. She took to the sport like a duck to water and within a year, in Manchester in 1993, became a junior world champion. The following year she was no longer a junior and competed in the female elite category of the world championships held in Wellington (there was as yet no under-23 category). She came 3rd in a stellar field.

Soon after, the ITU dropped the non-drafting rule and Sarah lost interest, as running was not her strongest discipline. For athletes like her, the rule change allowing competitors to bike in groups created a significant disadvantage. She was not the only one to quit the sport and the change saw a revival of the half ironman and ironman distance, which maintained the non-drafting rule. Sarah was not interested in the longer distances and retired too young.

Debbie Nelson – a duathlete at a time when the duathlon (run-bike-run) was still a respectable business – was the consummate professional. She was an accountant by trade with a background in middle-distance running and an aversion to water, so the run-bike-run was it.

Most runners take to biking well and so did Debbie. She trained diligently and placed consistently at world cups and world championship events. But the big one, a win at the world long-distance championships held every year in Zofingen, Switzerland, eluded her. She placed 3rd on three occasions. We decided she needed a change in approach and therefore coach. One year later in 1999, under the guidance of Scott Molina (a previous winner of the race, in 1991), she won the prestigious event.

>>>

The Terminator

The coach doesn't always get it right. Early in 1988, I got a phone call from Scott Molina, asking for advice about his preparation for the Hawaii Ironman later that year. Scott's nickname was 'The Terminator', as he raced a lot and won more races than any of his competitors. He was the only one left of the 'big four' who had never won this event (the others were Dave Scott, Scott Tinley and Mark Allen).

Scott is one of those people who break out in a sweat just getting out of a chair, which means that his physiology is not suited to competing for a prolonged time in the heat. Perspiring when competing in hot conditions is good, as it is an efficient way of getting rid of body heat. But if you sweat too much it becomes difficult to replace the lost fluid. Our stomach can process about 600ml of water or sports drink an hour. Some athletes can increase this to a litre by training their stomach to tolerate more, but an athlete like Scott easily loses more than a litre of sweat each hour, making it impossible for him to replace the loss over time.

I said as much to him: 'Scott, some athletes, like Dave Scott, are made for competing in the heat. They have a very efficient fluid balance. They perspire enough to keep the body cool, but not so much that the body is at risk of dehydration. You are not one of these athletes.' I was telling him indirectly not to waste his time on trying to win the Hawaii Ironman.

But Scott didn't heed my advice. He trained in Palm Springs for a couple of weeks prior to the race, under the blazing sun, filling himself up with salt before and during his long training sessions. Salt holds the water in the body. He would return with his body and bike caked in white from the high concentration of salt in his sweat. And it worked. He defied his physiology by clever manipulation through his salt-loading regime and – combined with a tremendous amount of willpower and determination – that won him the race.

I consider his win in 1988 one of the great feats in the history of triathlon.[1] In 2018 Scott Molina was inducted into the Ironman Hall of Fame. But the strategy was not sustainable. Scott's physiology never fell for the salt trick again; he tried to repeat his win in subsequent years, only to join the majority by imploding in the heat and finishing out of contention or not at all.

Watson and Bright

In 1994 the Olympic Committee announced that triathlon would be included in the 2000 Sydney Olympics. Within five years of establishing the International Triathlon Union, Les McDonald had achieved his goal for triathlon to be given Olympic status.

Craig Watson was 18 years old when in 1989 he joined our triathlon squad in Christchurch. I predicted he would become a good age-group athlete; he fitted the formula of limited potential multiplied by hard work equals age-group success. But Craig had other ideas. He was a quiet, unassuming young man, with deep-set eyes and gapped front teeth emphasised by a permanent boyish grin, which distracted observers from a hidden steely resolve. He trained harder and more consistently than any athlete I had coached, and became living proof that with consistent work over time you can achieve a lot, even if the potential seems limited.

For years he was mediocre, but over time he improved ever so slowly, inch by inch. From 1994, he travelled to Europe every year, trying to draw the attention of the French clubs, which ran a lucrative national competition. He didn't succeed in the first year. He slept under bridges and lived on the bones of his backside to get by. The next year he joined a second division club.

He worked his way up the rankings until he was noticed by the selectors back home in New Zealand and was invited to race for his country in world cup events. Two years out from the games it became clear that Craig was going to be a contender for a place in the first ever New Zealand Olympic triathlon team. He was not the only one amongst the athletes I was coaching.

Ben Bright was born in Waiuku, a small township located at the southern end of the Waiuku River, an estuarial arm of Auckland's Manukau Harbour. Ben's father is a Kiwi and his mother Australian. The family moved to Australia when Ben was 12, as job opportunities for his parents in Waiuku were few and far between. When Ben became a triathlete he chose to represent New Zealand as a junior at the 1990 Commonwealth Games in Auckland, at the age of 16. However, his parents could not afford to keep sending him to New Zealand for selection races and much to his displeasure he was forced to represent Australia in subsequent years. In 1994 he won the Junior World Championships title, competing under the Australian flag in Wellington.

Under the guidance of legendary coach Brett Sutton, Ben's workload and ambition exceeded his maturity and development.

He trained like a demon and competed mostly in the senior ranks against more mature athletes, matching them stride-for-stride and often beating them. Symptoms of burnout were the inevitable consequence and Ben disappeared from the international circuit for some time. In 1998, when he was 24, he decided to give it one last shot and try to qualify for the Olympic triathlon in Sydney two years later, but the Australian selectors were no longer interested in the struggling youngster. He contacted Graham Park, convenor of the Triathlon New Zealand selection committee, to see whether he could race for New Zealand. 'I feel 100% Kiwi,' he told Graham, hoping that would bolster his application.

Two years earlier, in 1996, to help us prepare for the Sydney Olympic Games, Graham Park, Terry Sheldrake and I had established the New Zealand Triathlon Academy.[2] A burned-out athlete from another country didn't strike me as a good contribution to the programme. I felt we had enough depth with home-grown athletes like Hamish Carter, Cameron Brown, Jamie Hunt, Craig Watson, Paul Amy and Shane Reed. Youngsters Kris Gemmell and Bevan Docherty were already showing promise for the future.

But Graham disagreed. He had a reputation for helping athletes in trouble. He promised it would not cost us any money until Ben had proven himself worthy of inclusion. In the end, I shrugged my shoulders and agreed.

Next morning, Ben called me from the Gold Coast. I could hear from his voice that he was not well. He suffered from chronic fatigue, he explained. 'Graham told me you're a sports doctor, so I thought perhaps you can help me.' I made the mistake of saying that the distance made that a bit difficult. Before I knew it, he was knocking on the front door of our home in Christchurch. Apart from his chronic fatigue, he was also broke, having spent the last of his money on the airfare. We took him in, initially for a few days, until he could get himself sorted. He left 18 months later, effectively an adopted member of our family.

All the training and racing with the big boys when he was still a junior had wrecked Ben's immune system and we kept having to compromise on his training, which went against his nature. Every time we pushed, he got sick.

The 2000 Sydney Olympics

Qualification for the 2000 Olympics took place at the World Cup event held in Sydney, a few months before the Games. The race was held on the Olympic course, and everybody was there, as it was a selection event for most countries. A top-five finish secured automatic Olympic selection for any of the New Zealand contenders.

Our team was headed by Hamish Carter. He was ranked number one in the world, was in tremendous shape and was favourite to win the race. His place in the top five was considered by many to be a certainty. Besides Hamish, the squad included Ben, Shane Reed, Craig Watson, Jamie Hunt and up-and-coming hotshot Kris Gemmell, who had earned a last-minute start. I coached Craig, Ben and Kris. Ben was tolerated by the other athletes only because they were aware of his medical predicament. He had not performed well for a long time, so was not considered a threat.

In the World Cup race, the field came out of the water in a long uninterrupted line. Small bunches formed on the bike, all within sight of each other. Gradually, the different packs came together. Ben was fit, but he needed a bit of a buffer for the run to have a chance to get that top five. There was no buffer that day, however. More than 50 athletes raced as one into the bike-to-run transition in a cacophony of screeching brakes and near crashes. Ben and

Craig Watson came out of the transition chaos side-by-side, sharing 5th and 6th place. It was mesmerising to watch the two running never more than 10m apart for the entire race. Neither was willing to give an inch, with Ben in front, desperate to get rid of his opponent, but Craig refusing to give in. It was a battle of wills. In the end, Ben beat Craig by a whisker in an all-out sprint.

Ben's 5th place was an automatic ticket to the Sydney Olympics. As the underdog and rank outsider amongst the Kiwis, he was the first to qualify. Hamish had a bad day and finished 32nd, while Jamie ran himself into 8th place from the rear of the field. Shane Reed, also thought to be a sure contender, finished 23rd.

The athletes who missed out had another chance to qualify for the two remaining spots two weeks later at the ITU World Championships in Perth. Ben was in bed for two weeks after his heroics; he would not have made the start-line in Perth.

Jamie Hunt had a better swim in Perth and was in the front bunch on the bike, together with Craig, Shane and Hamish. On paper, Jamie was the best runner, just ahead of Hamish, but Craig was tough. Shane was struggling with his form. In the final lap on the bike, disaster struck. Jamie's rear wheel slipped from under him in a tight corner and Craig, sitting on his wheel, had nowhere to go. They went down hard. Jamie got up first and threw his cut-up body onto his bike to set off in pursuit. Craig took a while longer, his handlebars sticking out at unhealthy angles.

Hamish had missed the carnage and scraped home in 5th to only just claim his Olympic berth. Jamie, Craig and Shane finished 11th, 27th and 30th respectively. As they had finished outside the qualifying criteria, our third Olympic spot was to be decided at the discretion of the selectors. I was one of those selectors, but as Craig's coach I had to withdraw from the panel. Eventually, Craig got the nod, which I deemed a controversial decision because of Jamie's running prowess. Jamie accepted the decision gracefully.

>>>

Ben was in the shape of his life one week out from the Olympics. The previous week, he had won the tough, 100km Christchurch-to-Akaroa bike race in convincing style against some of New Zealand's top professional cyclists. The weekend before the Olympic race, we decided to hold back a little and replace the planned bike race with a controlled training time trial over the Short Bays bike course around the hilly roads of the Port Hills. He improved his best time over the course by two minutes, which had not been in the plan. Next morning when I got up, I found him lying on the sofa in the living room, his eyes sunken in a gaunt, pale face. A few words between us confirmed the overnight return of his symptoms of chronic fatigue.

This happened every now and then, usually when we had pushed a bit too hard. Normally, it would take at least two weeks to get over. Bad timing. One week with little training gave us a glimmer of hope, however, as he started to feel better towards the end of it. We decided he could compete.

It was excruciating to watch him struggle over the course. 'I had nothing, John,' he said after the race. He didn't finish last – that honour was reserved for Dutch veteran Rob Barel, who waved to the crowd as if he had won the race. But Ben's 38th place felt like last for the athlete and the coach.

Ben went missing in action from the Olympic village for 10 days following the race. If you ask him what he did in those 10 days he'll tell you he has no recollection whatsoever, so it remains a mystery.[3]

>>>

Craig finished first New Zealander, in 16th place. At our debrief following the race, he taught me a valuable lesson. At the time, he was fifth in world rankings and in very good shape; a podium place or at least top eight had not been unrealistic, and I told him as much. He gave me a friendly smile. 'John, I gave it everything,' he said. 'I had stomach issues during the run, but I never gave up. I'm happy, because I know God is happy as I've given it my best. Not to do my best is disrespectful to God and others I care about and I know that I have done everything I could, so I'm at peace with the result.'

I often quote this story to athletes when the outcome of their race does not meet their expectations. They can be happy as long as they know they have done everything to the best of their ability (regardless of their religious beliefs). There can't be any argument against that and it takes the heat out of feelings of disappointment.

Craig's secret for exceeding expectations and becoming an accomplished elite athlete was not only hard work. His religion and an unyielding faith in God, who he felt supported him in his journey as long as he did his best, gave him great strength. It gave him the calm confidence many athletes crave. Describing to me the importance of his faith during his athletic career, he explained: 'The reason the notion of effort is so important to me is because I hold myself 100% responsible to God for my actions. Because I am responsible for my own actions, I can't use God or my faith or "destiny" as an excuse for doing or not doing anything, which is what fundamentalists and extremists do.'

A few months after the Sydney Olympics, Craig confirmed his world ranking by winning bronze medals at the Edmonton ITU World Championships and the now-defunct Goodwill Games in Brisbane.

Sore shins plagued Craig for a large part of his career. He was not really built for running, as his legs were not only short but also alarmingly bowed – you could sail a schooner through the space between his knees. Craig's unfortunate anatomy combined with his relentless training regime were the main cause of ongoing stress fractures in his shinbones. He listened to me politely when I suggested he take a break from running for a while to let his legs heal. He asked if it could do him long-term harm if he kept running. I had to admit that was unlikely. He upped his training with renewed vigour.

Towards the end of his career, Craig came to see me. 'John, I want to pay you some money for all the coaching you've done,' he said. I had never charged him, as he always seemed to be broke. Besides, I considered myself more a friend and adviser than his coach. He often wrote his own training programmes, especially when he was overseas, and I have already made it clear who his real coach was.

But I was happy with his offer as by then the other athletes I coached were paying me something, so I felt his proposition was also fair to them. I suggested that he pay me 10% of his prize money. He paused for a moment and his permanent grin suddenly left him, making way for seriousness.

'John, I can't do that, because I already pay 10% of my income to the church. If I pay you the same amount, I put you on the same level as God.'

All I could say was that I had no intention of competing with God. 'Mate, I'd be on a hiding to nothing, so just pay me what you think it's worth.' We left it at that and never broached the subject again. I'd like to think that Craig and his super coach, the Lord Almighty, will have a bit of a chuckle when they read this.

Kris Gemmell: Wonderboy

If I ever had to go to war and had a choice of companion, I would choose Kris Gemmell. Why? Because he would know when to duck. Not only that, he'd also warn me, even if he got down well before me. He's everything I am not and vice versa, which has led to some challenging times for athlete and coach during the 12 years of our partnership.

Kris came to Christchurch from Palmerston North in 1996 as an 18-year-old fresh from school and with a dream of becoming a professional triathlete. He was lean, almost scrawny, with a permanent grin etched on a delicate face, restless eyes and signs of a receding hairline, even then.

He had played on the wing for the Manawatu Rugby development team, but decided he got pummelled too much. He was fast. His muscles have a lot of fast-twitch fibres, which combined with the fast-twitch neurons in his brain was potentially a killer combination, especially if we could change some of the muscle fibres into slow-twitch and tell his brain to be patient.[4] So, we got to work.

Initially things didn't go well. Kris cut corners in training or didn't show up, usually with an excuse you couldn't dispute. With a personality bordering on ADHD and a street-wise brain to go with it, he talked a lot and often spoke in riddles, so his responses kept me on my toes over the years. Others found the same – we called it 'Gemmellism' or 'Gemmellisation'. Kris seemed oblivious and didn't understand when we teased him about it. It was just who he was; the way he spoke was the way he thought.

He had been in Christchurch only three months when I had to tell him to go back to Palmerston North because he was too disruptive for the rest of the squad. I didn't think I would see him again, but he was back after a couple of months, asking for a second chance.

His attitude had improved, and the fact that he had returned made me decide to put more work into him. Kris was fast, but he didn't have a big engine. When we first began training, he would 'die' 600m into the swim, 15km into the bike ride, and 4km into the run. With a lot of strength-endurance work, we were able to gradually delay the time he blew, until in the end he could go the distance without having to slow down too much.

As noted earlier, Kris got his start in the selection race for the Sydney Olympics at the eleventh hour. He was on the waiting list and turned up for the race not knowing if he was going to be able to start. One hour before the start the transition area was closed, and one of the competitors had not turned up, so Kris was given his spot. He had a good swim and made a small leading bunch, only to be outsmarted by a fellow competitor on a tricky bend. Kris had nowhere to go and crashed out of the race.

Four years later he also missed out on selection for the Athens Olympic Games. Hamish Carter and Bevan Docherty were the top dogs and they had already qualified, while Kris was right behind them on number three ranking. We hadn't counted on Hamish Carter preferring Nathan Richmond as an Olympic training partner. Hamish had worked out a plan, and helped Nathan escape from the bike bunch during the final Olympic selection race. Kris had to do all the chasing and in the end he ran out of road. It was a blow for us. Nathan had never beaten Kris (and would never beat him again). However, Kris being Kris, he still joined Bevan, Hamish and Nathan to assist them with their preparation for the Olympics.

Bevan Docherty summed him up: 'Kris's problem is he's always so helpful and has made so many sacrifices for others. I'm selfish, but Kris can't be like that, and it's probably been detrimental to him.' Bevan hit the nail on the head. In the daily functioning of society, selflessness is a most commendable personality trait, but it's deadly in the brutal environment of high-performance sport. Kris's consolation prize, soon after the 2004 Athens Olympics, was winning his first ITU World Cup race in Gamagori, Japan.

I was in the Netherlands during the Athens Olympics and watched the men's triathlon race unfold on the television screen in amazement. Too nervous to sit still, I was on my indoor bike trainer. I raced alongside the boys over the bike course and was right next to them on the run. I nearly fell off my stationary bike when they got to the sprint finish – gold for Hamish and silver for Bevan. Who would have thought that before the race?

The Athens experience meant we were very motivated to get it right for Beijing. Kris knew that on his good days he was the equal of his Athens gold- and silver-medal buddies. He was going to be 31 at the Beijing Olympics and potentially in the best shape of his career.

In late 2004, he partnered with Anja Dittmer, one of the stars of the German triathlon team, and managed to talk himself into the inner sanctum of the German training centre in Saarbrücken. He ate, trained and socialised with the German athletes, and from then on returned to Saarbrücken during the New Zealand winters. I don't think the stern Germans quite knew what to do with this flighty Kiwi. I hoped some of the German discipline and structure would rub off on him.

Kris asked me to continue writing his training schedules while he was in Germany, which I dutifully did. He said the German boys liked to train with him, so I might for all those years have unwittingly been training the German team, which included

Jan Frodeno, the 2008 Beijing Olympic champion. I suspect Kris may have been one of those athletes who had three training programmes: the first, the one that I wrote for him; the second, the one that he executed; and the third, the programme that he sometimes wrote down in his training diary. I assumed the Germans knew what they were doing, as Germans generally do. The arrangement seemed to work, as he came out of these training camps firing on all cylinders.

Kris also spent time with his mate Bevan Docherty, which I encouraged because I felt Kris could learn from Bevan's toughness and ruthlessness. The plan was structure and discipline from the Germans, resilience from Bevan and a bit of oversight from me. In time he became a 'podium' athlete, often in contention and even on the winner's dais a couple of times: he won the World Aquathlon Championships in 2002 and came 4th at the Lausanne World Championships in 2006. He had a lot of setbacks, sometimes self-inflicted, but he also had some bad luck when fate just seemed to go against him. He would never fret long after disappointments, because that was not in his nature. This, together with his cheerfulness, made him an endearing character and a popular squad member.

Kris needed to qualify in the top eight at the World Cup held in Beijing in the year prior to the 2008 Olympics. Bevan had already qualified. Hamish had retired. Shane Reed and Terenzo Bozzone were the other two New Zealand contenders in the hunt for qualification. The race went well for Kris. He was always near the front, and 3km from the finish he was running next to two of his mates, Bevan Docherty and the Australian Courtney Atkinson. They were going to fight out the minor placings, as leader Javier Gomez from Spain was well out of sight.

Then something curious happened. As they approached the finish line, they split and Courtney moved ahead of Bevan and Kris. It was obvious Bevan was not trying and Kris looked as if he was out for a jog. I did not understand. After celebrating his Olympic qualification, I asked Kris what happened. 'Mate, you don't want to know,' he said. Of course, this 'Gemmellism' made me even more curious and I pressed him. Okay, they'd done a deal.

'What sort of a deal?'

Courtney had to be in the top two to earn automatic selection for Australia. As they approached the finish line, he asked Bevan and Kris if he could have that second spot behind Gomez. Bevan was fine with it, and Kris only needed a top eight for his Olympic qualification. And so the deal was done and three of them got what they wanted – Courtney 2nd, Bevan 3rd and Kris 4th. At first, I was absolutely stunned; then I became furious and gave Kris a good old bollocking: 'You looked the strongest of the three and didn't put up a fight for second place just to do your mates a favour?' I couldn't believe it. Kris just shrugged his shoulders and said I needed to grow up – this was professional sport. But for once his usual cheeky grin had disappeared. It was the first and only time he showed exasperation with his coach's deficiencies.

It was also the moment when it hit me that I did not want to do this anymore. Although they had done nothing illegal, to me their tactics went against the spirit of our sport, any sport for that matter, except perhaps professional cycling, where doing deals is the order of the day. I decided I would take a break from coaching after the Beijing Olympics.

>>>

Andrea Hewitt: Noise

Contrary to current practice, I have not been in the habit of poaching potential triathletes from other sporting codes. Andrea Hewitt was the one exception. In her late teens, she was already a multiple national age-group swim and surf lifesaving champion, with the ironman her favourite event.

The surf lifesaving ironman first appeared in Australia in 1964, well before triathlon hijacked the name for the first Hawaii event in 1978, and combines four main disciplines of swimming, board paddling, running and ski paddling into a single event. The three water-based disciplines in and out of the surf are transitioned by a short beach run. The event only takes 10 to 20 minutes, but challenging surf conditions usually make it into a gruelling affair deserving of the name. The winners are considered true heroes and the surf lifesaving version of the ironman boasts some of the fittest all-round athletes on the planet.

Andrea could already swim and run with the best. As her sports doctor at the time, I followed her career with interest. In addition to a surf lifesaving background and a competitive spirit, she had the ideal physical build for triathlon – small, light and lean of stature. She had never ridden a bike in her life, but that could be easily remedied. She was 21 when I casually suggested she do a triathlon.

Andrea rejected the suggestion rather bluntly. I learned she is a fiercely loyal person, and she was not going to give up on 'her' sport, which was also a family affair, as she often competed alongside her sisters, Tina and Sara.

'Let me know when you're ready,' were my parting words.

Two years later, in late 2004, she came knocking on my door. That year, the national surf lifesaving selectors had left her off the national team in favour of other athletes. Andrea has a strong sense of fairness and she felt betrayed. Surf lifesaving's loss became triathlon's gain.

But there was one more obstacle to overcome. 'First, I want to do the Coast to Coast,' she said. I despaired. New Zealand's biggest multisport race, the Coast to Coast, takes competitors from Kumara on the West Coast of the South Island, across the rugged Southern Alps to Christchurch on the east coast, a stretch of 247km. At least 100 of those kilometres are done off-road via a 30km mountain run and a 70km kayak leg down the grade-two Waimakariri River. It's a race with a difference, crossing some of the wildest terrain and the most beautiful scenery in the world. It is one of the toughest endurance races on offer and is often called the multisport equivalent of the ironman triathlon. Not a logical start for a budding triathlete, in my books.

I had no say in it, though, as Andrea had already entered the one-day event, with three months to prepare. On the day, she found the 30km mountain run a far cry from the short beach sprints she was used to. The lead-in 50km bike ride had already fatigued her untrained legs. Her short stature didn't help with the multiple river crossings and boulder-hopping sections. I was pleased when I got news she had come out of that section of the race intact, albeit bruised and battered.

While the majority of competitors use specially designed racing kayaks, Andrea used a small kayak similar to her surf ski for the 70km down-river section. She soon discovered the difference when other competitors shot past her on the flatter river sections. At least her smaller kayak helped her to stay upright through the treacherous rapids.

Being new to cycling, she was still scared of bunch riding and kept a safe distance from other riders, wasting unnecessary energy.

It says a lot that she still managed to finish 4th woman, which, considering her inexperience, was a formidable achievement. She said afterwards it was the hardest thing she had ever done.

Two weeks later she did her first proper triathlon. It was the national championships, and she finished 4th overall and 3rd in the under-23 category. She ran with the leaders until 3km from the finish, when she blew to bits. I felt she would have won the race if she hadn't wasted her time with the Coast to Coast, as it was clear to me that she had not fully recovered. I was happy with the outcome, however, as it was more likely she would now take notice of her coach. She did, and with five more months of cycling under her belt later that year, she convincingly won the world under-23 triathlon championships in Gamagori, Japan.

Andrea's nickname was 'Noise', because she never said much, which was difficult at times when I needed some feedback. I had to pull it out of her. To questions like 'How do you feel?' or 'What do you think?' I would get a monosyllabic answer or a shrug of her shoulders. The only time she got excited was when I asked after her family; she would chatter away like a sparrow in a tree. She seemed generally contented, with triathlon and her family her main interests. We got on well.

In 2006 Andrea won a bronze medal at the Melbourne Commonwealth Games, in a sprint finish with team-mate Debbie Tanner, who had caught her with 1km to go. I was right there when Debbie passed Andrea. It was obvious that Andrea had hit the wall, still inexperienced in pace judgement and lacking the training years to be able to go full bore all the way. Her face was gaunt, her eyes expressionless and her legs wobbly. She hesitated a moment when her team-mate came past, then I saw her back straighten and her legs start to turn over a fraction faster. With one final effort, she closed the small gap and carried on to win the sprint for the bronze medal by less than a second. That's not something you can coach; some athletes just have the ability to push that little bit harder than anyone else at crucial times.

Andrea won her first World Cup event in Kitzbühel, Austria, a year later. It was a memorable occasion because Nicky Samuels, who I also coached, came 3rd. Next, Andrea set her sights on selection for the Beijing Olympics. Her aim was a top eight at the World Cup event in Beijing. She crashed her bike in training at high speed a couple of months out, which hampered her preparation, and she finished 14th. Debbie Tanner and Sam Warriner secured their selections by finishing 4th and 6th.

The Mooloolaba World Cup in March 2008 was Andrea's last chance to secure the third spot on the team. She had to finish in the top six, but this time her preparation was affected by illness and once again she finished 14th. There was no doubt she was the best of the rest; she had not been beaten by the two other contenders, Evelyn Williamsen and Nicky Samuels. She was offered the third spot subject to her agreeing to be the domestique[5] for Sam and Debbie, both vulnerable in the swim. Not agreeing would mean no Olympics, so she shrugged her shoulders and accepted, knowing she would have the better of the two anyway if she was fully fit.

When Andrea switched from surf lifesaving to triathlon she remained loyal to her swim coach, Roly Crichton. She still trains under him every New Zealand summer, when she comes home to recuperate from the Northern Hemisphere season, see her family and prepare for the upcoming season. Under Roly her swimming gets back up to the level it needs to be to remain competitive.

Roly Crichton

Roly was one of the first New Zealand swim coaches to take triathletes seriously. He worked out the special requirements for open-water swimming in a crowd and applied this to his training methods. Where pool swimmers typically aim for an even or negative split, triathletes need to be at the first buoy near the front of the group to avoid the chaos which invariably occurs when 60 swimmers converge on the same spot almost all at once. Preparing for that requires a special approach in training and Roly understood that; indeed, he revelled in the challenge. Today Roly is best known for guiding international superstar para swimmer Sophie Pascoe to multiple Olympic and world titles.

Roly is also known for his colourful personality. There's a misconception that he was nicknamed Roly because he moves around in a wheelchair, but actually his first name is Ronald, which was shortened to Roly by his mates well before his accident.

Roly was brought up in foster homes and grew up with the wrong crowd, becoming an angry and violent youth. One day in 1976, when he was 17, he was in a car with his mates, heading home from the pub. Roly was in the back. There were no seatbelts for back seats then, and no one took much notice of drink-driving laws. The car was speeding and the driver lost control, the car rolled over twice and came to rest upside down in a shallow creek beside the road.

The four boys crawled out through the windows, dazed. They checked each other out. In a drunken stupor Roly mumbled that he had a sore back. His mates dragged him to the side of the road, where, just before he drifted into unconsciousness, he swore and whispered that now he also couldn't feel his legs.

Roly woke up in the spinal ward of Christchurch Hospital, and was told he would never walk again. The accident did nothing to dispel his deep feeling of anger with the world. He soon discharged himself and, through trial and error and with help from other paraplegics, he learned the basics of how to get by in a wheelchair. He drifted for a while, felt sorry for himself, and suffered from self-neglect, resulting in repeated hospital admissions.

Somewhere along the line he discovered swimming, first as a means for rehabilitation, later as a way of getting respect from his peers that didn't involve the use of his fists. Roly was powerful and he excelled in the 50m freestyle. His swimming was fast and furious, like his personality. He broke the world record and won a gold medal over his favourite distance at the 1984 Stoke Mandeville Paralympics, and another gold at the Paralympics in Seoul in 1988. His wild streak got him into trouble a lot. At the 1983 World Championships at Stoke Mandeville he knocked out a competitor suspected of attempting to rape a female volunteer, and in transit to the 1984 Paralympics he lashed out at the team manager and broke three of his ribs.

But the hours Roly spent training in the pool provided him with a lot of time to think. In time he realised he had an opportunity to do something with his life apart from beating people up. One day he confided to me that the accident was the best thing that could have happened to him. When I asked him why, he said he would otherwise be in prison or dead.

When he retired from swimming, he became a coach and had an immediate affinity with youngsters. He learned very quickly and soon had success with his swimmers. His hard-nosed attitude remained, but most of the time he was able to channel his aggressiveness into his job – although he never completely lost his rough edges and had regular arguments and fall-outs with administrators and other coaches.

Roly is a coach from the same mould as Arthur Lydiard and Duncan Laing, both intuitive coaches, using their experience, personal beliefs and gut feeling to guide their athletes to success. Around the turn of the 21st century, coaches started to use sports science – measuring and monitoring heart rate, power output, sweat rate, blood lactate and much more – to optimise training, racing and recovery. Most modern coaches have access to biomechanists, physiologists, nutritionists, psychologists, doctors and physiotherapists. As long as the input of these experts is managed carefully and the coach remains in charge, this multi-disciplinary model can be very effective. In reality most coaches use a combination of experience, instinct and science in their coaching. Science has its limitations and the best coaches are still the ones who use their gut feeling when having to make instantaneous decisions under pressure.

Roly eventually came to realise that coaching had progressed from the days of Lydiard and Laing; he had to adjust to the modern way if he wanted to survive in the high-performance environment. He consulted experts and other coaches and soaked up the information they gave him. He went to seminars, courses and workshops to learn about leadership and the sport's scientific disciplines. Over time, he has become not only a better coach but also a more content human being.

Sometimes, though, he can't help himself and reverts to the old Roly. Recently, when a young triathlete who was struggling to keep up asked Roly how she could improve, he growled that she should rip her head off and replace it with a cabbage, before wheeling away.

The Dunedin years, 2002–2009

In 2002, Ien was appointed as a lecturer at the Human Nutrition Department of the University of Otago in Dunedin. At first she commuted between Christchurch and Dunedin – a five-hour drive – so she only came home for the weekends. I didn't like it, so in 2004 I sold out of my medical practice and we moved to Dunedin, where we bought a small cottage at Waitati, on the shores of Blueskin Bay, north of the city. I divided my time between coaching, a small sports-medicine practice, and a job as lecturer in sports medicine and exercise prescription at the University of Otago.

The Otago coastline is one of the most pristine in the world, with an abundance of wildlife – sea lions, seals, penguins and a number of seabirds, including the royal albatross. I'm sure the only reason why that particular part of New Zealand is not over-populated is because all year round a bone-chilling wind blows in straight from the South Pole. Winters are freezing cold and there is no summer to speak of.

I didn't mind. I loved training and competing in the wild and lonely landscapes around Dunedin in all kinds of weather. The bike races around the backblocks of the Taieri Plains were notorious for serving up lashings of cold and misery. Sharing this with fellow competitors made it not only tolerable but even enjoyable at times – particularly afterwards, when defrosting in the pub.

>>>

Duncan Laing

Moana Pool is the main swimming pool in Dunedin. It was home to legendary swim coach Duncan Laing (1933–2008), who produced more New Zealand swimming champions than you can throw a stick at. His most famous pupil was double Olympic gold medallist Danyon Loader.

Associate Professor Dave Gerrard – the same Dave Gerrard I had competed against in the Dunedin quadrathlon in 1984 – was my boss at the university. He had trained under Laing as a swimmer. Dave showed me 'his' pool early one morning before we swam our customary lengths, and offered to introduce me to Duncan. Excited about finally meeting this living legend, I was led to the 25m training pool, where the swimmers were busy doing their laps.

Duncan was a giant of a man, not only by reputation but also physically. He was as wide as he was tall. He was sitting poolside on a bench, arms crossed in front of a huge chest, his head hung low, chin resting on his chest. At first I thought he was carefully studying the swimmers, but then I realised he was fast asleep. 'Don't wake him up,' I pleaded, alarmed about the consequences if we did. Duncan's health was known to be fragile.

We were standing a few metres away from him, chatting, all the while keeping an eye on the master coach. His arms rose rhythmically on his huge chest. 'He's not going to wake up in a hurry,' I thought. But just as we were about to retreat, I saw one eye open, then another. Suddenly, with surprising speed and agility, Duncan grabbed a kickboard lying next to him and threw it with all his might into the centre lane, where it hit one of the swimmers right between the eyes. The swimmer looked up and with shouts and gestures Duncan conveyed his instructions about hand entry into the water. The swimmer carried on and Duncan promptly went back to sleep. The whole scene took less than a few seconds.

It was the most masterful display of coaching I had ever seen. Dave saw my reaction of awe and laughed. He explained that Duncan used to be in the habit of flinging his car keys, but was eventually told it was too dangerous. Ever since, he'd used the kickboard instead – a different coaching tool – but with just as much accuracy.

A few months later, during a triathlon training camp where I was coaching a swim session, I tried the technique myself. One of the triathletes was annoying a swimmer in front of him. I picked up a kickboard and aimed it at the triathlete. The kickboard flew well off course, hitting the head of an unsuspecting elderly aqua jogger a few lanes along. She got the fright of her life and looked around, in shock. I quickly turned away to study the training session on the whiteboard, pretending innocence and ignorance. I have never tried it again.

The first thing I did when we moved to Dunedin was set up a triathlon squad so I could continue my coaching activities. There were plenty of takers, with a core of university students keen to give it a go, including Tony Dodds and Nicky Samuels. Tony competed at national level as a distance freestyle swimmer, but was looking for new challenges; Nicky had played hockey at national level, and for fun and as part of her fitness regime she had entered the world triathlon championships held in Queenstown the previous year (2003), coming second in her age group. When she approached me about coaching her, I said national-level hockey and big aspirations in triathlon were not good bedfellows, so she had to choose. She chose triathlon.

Nicky lived up to her promise as an age grouper. She laughed and giggled a lot, but underneath all that she was tough. That, combined with a love for hard work, saw her quickly progress through the ranks. She finished a close third at the 2006 world championships in Lausanne, behind Australians Erin Densham and Emma Moffatt in the elite under-23 category.

Nicky was never able to improve as much as Erin and Emma did, largely as a result of mysterious symptoms that forced her to slow down at crucial times when competing, usually during the run. She was finally diagnosed with arrhythmia (irregular heart beat), something that's not uncommon in endurance athletes but which is sometimes hard to diagnose – there are many types, with a bewildering variety of symptoms, the cause of which is not always clear.[6] Nicky had a heart-rate monitor implanted under her skin that recorded an electro-cardiographic reading of her heart rate every second for six months, which finally confirmed the diagnosis.

Over time, treatment has been only partially successful. Despite this, Nicky never gave up and stayed her happy but determined self. In 2013, she won the XTERRA World Championships, and she represented New Zealand at the London and Rio Olympics.

I would gladly have stayed in Dunedin. As well as loving the ruggedness and beauty of the unspoiled coastline (and not minding the weather), I had also discovered that the further south you travel in New Zealand the friendlier the folks. But Ien was homesick for her friends in Christchuch and she did not like the colder climate. She'd already uprooted once, moving to New Zealand, and did not want to 'emigrate' a second time, so we returned to Christchurch in 2009.

The 2008 Beijing Olympics

Meanwhile I had been putting all my coaching experience from the previous 25 years into the preparation of Andrea Hewitt and Kris Gemmell for the 2008 Beijing Olympics. Andrea was aiming for a top 10 and Kris for nothing less than a gold medal.

There are two types of coaches – those who surround themselves with experts and those who don't. I'm one of the former. My co-coaches included double-Olympic marathoner Pete Pfitzinger, who assisted with running programmes, and swim coach Andrew Nicholls, who had already transformed Kris from a mid-pack into a consistent front-pack swimmer. Other key experts I called on were my dietician wife Ien to assist with nutrition, and mental conditioner Renzie Hanham, who is an expert on performing under pressure.

The national programme, under high-performance director Stephen Farrell, had obtained funding to employ a sports scientist. Rob Creasy, an age-group triathlete and ambitious scientist (an excellent combination), was keen and eager, but Stephen was not sure what to do with him. So, I was able to snap him up for a while.

Until then I had used sports science in a haphazard manner. Rob made sure we applied some method to the sports science madness. In the lead-up to the Games, we used compression garments, respiratory muscle training, different forms of altitude training and simulation, specific strength-training techniques, heart rate variability monitoring and heat acclimatisation, to name a few. We also fine-tuned the inhalers Kris used for his exercise-induced asthma, essential for competing in the polluted Beijing air.[7] Last but not least, I proposed to Kris that we both undergo psychometric testing to improve our mutual understanding. Our relationship at the time was strained to the extent that we were drifting apart. The incident at the Olympic selection race the previous year had not helped. We were hanging on to each other like a bad habit, which was not good for the coach-athlete dynamic.

I suggested the testing to Kris during a bike ride, but he dismissed the idea. 'I'm not going to see a shrink,' was his curt reply. I had expected some reluctance, but not such a blunt rejection of the idea. But I had an ace up my sleeve. 'What if Fleur does it?' Fleur is my daughter, who, at the time, worked as a 'people development' specialist in a human resources company. Psychometric testing was her business. Kris knew Fleur well enough and trusted her. He agreed.

After the lengthy process of testing, Kris and I shut ourselves in a room together, comparing results. Not surprisingly, the analysis showed us to be complete opposites: Kris – extroverted, charming, energetic and independent, me – more introverted, quiet and reserved. At the end of the session, Kris pointed his finger at me, winked and exclaimed: 'Got you sussed, bro.' I had achieved my goal. The process of the exercise brought us closer together, with restored mutual respect.

I included a simplified version of our sports science support plan in Andrea's Olympic preparation. Psychometric testing was not required; we had an uncomplicated coach-athlete relationship. She was straightforward, tough, seldom complaining and compliant with the programme.

Andrea's Olympic build-up was interrupted by frequent illness and injury. Ten weeks out from the Games, she was still struggling. We had planned a training stint at Font-Romeu (1800m up in the Pyrenees in Southern France) to do some solid base training, before embarking on a more specific training block at sea level for the final six weeks.

It is a written rule that you do not take sick, injured or unfit athletes to altitude for training. Andrea was all of those. Was I going to leave her behind somewhere at sea level hoping she would come right or was I going to bring her up with us and take the risk? I decided on the latter. At least I would be right there beside her, and with the help of Rob Creasy we could monitor her closely.

High-altitude air has therapeutic qualities when managed carefully. Simply being exposed to it, even when you're sedentary, improves your fitness, due to the lower oxygen content of the inhaled air. For the first week, Andrea trained for short sessions and at a low intensity, and she responded immediately. She felt better, her resting heart rate came down rapidly and her heart-rate response during training improved with every passing day, together with her energy levels.

In the second and third weeks of the camp, I was able to give her some decent training sessions, and the day she came down from altitude she shared victory with Hollie Avil in a French Grand Prix. Hollie's coach Ben Bright and I acknowledged with a firm handshake the special moment of the two athletes crossing the finish line hand-in-hand.

We were now six weeks out from Andrea's Olympic race. The remainder of her build-up went according to plan, including a solid 4th placing at the Kitzbühel World Cup event.

>>>

Kris had a superb build-up in the months before the Olympics. Based in Saarbrücken in the spring, the feedback suggested he was on track for a good summer. He tolerated more training than at any other time. He won races – including the notorious Schliersee triathlon – and he achieved regular personal bests in training.

Our focus had been on his running strength. Kris was always where he needed to be at the 8km mark, but had difficulty finishing off. Some more targeted strength training would get him up another level, so I introduced him to sled running. I had seen rugby players pulling heavy sleds in training and I liked the concept. We used a much lighter weight, one that Kris could sustain at his 10km race pace for about 200m. He did sled repeats twice a week, and we maintained these sessions at altitude when we were at Font-Romeu. He had done so much altitude training by this stage in his career that for him these sessions were comparable to training at sea level.

Following his altitude stint, Kris competed in the men's race at the same French Grand Prix where Andrea had tied first with Hollie Avil. He won there, too, beating Tim Don and a whole lot of Olympic contenders, including his German mate, Jan Frodeno. Was this going to be the year for Kris? Two weeks later, he finished 2nd in the Kitzbühel World Cup behind the always unpredictable Spanish ex-world champion Iván Raña, but ahead of the silver and bronze medal winners from Athens, Bevan Docherty and Sven Riederer.

Ten days out from the Beijing Olympic race, Kris had one more event in his programme. It was a super-sprint race in Germany – a 300m swim, 15km bike ride and 3km run, held in Gelsenkirchen. It was meant to be a formality, a final sharpener, which he was not going to try to win. I went to Holland for a few days to see my family and planned to meet him the day following the race, in Frankfurt, for our departure to Jeju in South Korea, where we would join the other New Zealand athletes and coaches for our final preparations.

We had agreed he would call me after the race, so I was puzzled when I saw his name flash up on the screen of my mobile phone during race time. Kris was crying: 'Mate, something terrible has happened – I cut my foot.'

'Cut your foot? How the hell did you cut your foot?' I had visions of him stepping on a piece of glass or some other rubbish at the entry or exit to the swim. It had happened before.

He said he had a good swim and came out with the front pack, hopped on his bike, and hadn't yet got his feet into his shoes, when one of the guys swerved into him. Kris tried to avoid him, but his foot slipped from the top of the shoe into the front wheel. The bladed spoke cut him badly under the big toe, all the way to the bone.

Kris had a tendency to exaggerate and my first thought was that he was going to be okay. It was a bit of a cut. We could cope with that. But when he said he was in an ambulance on the way to hospital, I was alarmed. He called me again later that night. A plastic surgeon had sewn the wound up; the cut was between his first (big) and second toe, and extended well under the ball of his foot, exactly the area required for 'toeing off' when running.

Miraculously the deep cut had not severed any tendons, according to the surgeon, but there was some nerve damage. The latter was good news in my opinion, as it would numb some of the pain. The surgeon had evaded Kris's burning question of whether he could still compete at the Games. I could only say: 'That sounds not too bad. We can make that work.' But I knew in all likelihood we were going to have our work cut out.

Kris arrived at Frankfurt Airport in a wheelchair, looking pale and dejected, his right foot heavily bandaged. I had suggested he ask for an upgrade so he could elevate his injured foot during the flight to prevent swelling, but his request was declined because the plane was full. I started arguing with the ground staff, trying to get them to understand how serious this was, but they wouldn't budge. A Lufthansa pilot walked past. He asked what was going on. I explained the situation and he asked me curtly if I was the doctor. I nodded enthusiastically. Perhaps he would bow to the authority of a doctor's request. He said in a thick German accent: 'I do you a deal. We put him up in first class if the flight attendants can call on you as the official doctor for this flight.' I gratefully agreed, sure the responsibility would not be too onerous. I had attended mid-air emergencies before.

Kris disappeared to the front of the plane, while I settled into cattle class, not wanting to push our luck by asking for an extra first-class seat for the official in-flight doctor. It didn't take long to get my first emergency call; someone was feeling sick. Then another call, and another. They were coming thick and fast, all for minor ailments usually handled by the flight crew. I realised they had decided to make the best of my appointment as in-flight medic. I was called as soon as any passenger pressed the buzzer and expressed even a hint of a health concern. I spent the next nine hours taking pulses (about the only thing you can monitor while on a plane) and reassuring passengers they weren't going to die.

At one point I was called to attend to an incident that initially sounded quite serious. A young boy was lying in the aisle, apparently in a dead faint, his mother wailing hysterically. My guess is that what had started out as harmless attention seeking had earned him a whole lot more attention than he'd wanted; alarmed by his mother's over-reaction and the consternation of the crew he'd had no choice but to keep up the act, squeezing his eyes tight shut and no doubt wishing we would all go away, but instead it had escalated into a near-emergency. An unforeseen icy stopover in Siberia was almost on the cards (which would have been disastrous for Kris' foot and our schedule) as the captain offered to divert the flight to the nearest airport, but I assured him that there was most definitely no need for that. (I had assessed the boy's consciousness with a slap on his face, which was accepted practice then – these days it's done by pinching the skin.) I dispensed a quiet but stern word in the boy's ear and the dose of tough love had an instant effect. Miraculously recovered, he quickly got up and scuttled back to his seat with his mother. Crisis averted.

A creaky old van without air-conditioning took us from the airport to Jeju. When we arrived, I organised an urgent meeting with the coaches and management. I told them I expected Kris to be fit to race on the day. The question of whether he should be replaced by Terenzo Bozzone, who was the official reserve, never came up. We devised an intensive rehabilitation plan of preventive antibiotics, daily clean, debride and dressing of the wound and daily hyperbaric treatment.

I found a one-person hyperbaric chamber in a regional hospital two hours' drive from where we were staying. Hyperbaric air is the opposite of the hypobaric air you find at altitude. Hyperbaric air contains a higher concentration of small oxygen molecules that penetrate deeper and faster into the body due to the increased air pressure. When more oxygen is available, the damaged tissue heals more quickly.

The hospital itself was a chaotic hive of activity. Corridors and wards were overflowing with patients, visitors and staff. Outside the main entrance, a great number of patients gathered in their pyjamas for a smoke, many still attached to their intravenous lines. That was ironic, as the hospital specialised in the treatment of lung cancer.

Unfortunately, Kris suffers from claustrophobia and the one-person hyperbaric chamber was like a small enclosed coffin. After he was zipped into the unit, a view through a small window was the only contact we had. When Kris eyeballed me through this little window, I could see he'd turned pale green with fear. Droplets of perspiration on his forehead soon turned into rivers. I laughed. He gave me the one-fingered salute. He spent an hour in the chamber every day for eight days.

Initially, we replaced running with aqua running, since Kris was unable to run with the stitches still in place. We did this in the sea off the coast near Tongyeong – illegally, as we soon found out when the local police arrived in force, their patrol car lights flashing. They stood on the cliff waving their batons, which were also equipped with flashing lights. Pete Pfitzinger, one of the other coaches, distracted them by spinning a long story while Kris and I completed the workout in the deep, well off the coast.

I took the stitches out after five days, which was five days earlier than the doctor had ordered. My hands trembled while I did this, waiting for the wound to burst open. It didn't. Kris had his first tentative run the next day.

>>>

The women's race at the Beijing Games was up first. Andrea's result was a gutsy 8th. She ran well above her ability for the first 3km, shoulder-to-shoulder with the eventual winner, Australian Emma Snowsill. She explained later: 'This was the Olympics. I was happy to take the risk and throw everything at it.' She did it tough for the second half of the run, drifting back through the field.

Before the race, we had agreed on a conservative start to the run, in view of the tough course and conditions. For once she had deviated from the agreed tactics. If she had paced herself a bit more sensibly she would have finished in 5th or 6th place. But in the end, I could only admire her courageous approach.

Laurent Vidal: Life after life

I first met French triathlete Laurent Vidal at the 2007 Triathlon World Cup event in Beijing where I was coach to Kris Gemmell and Andrea Hewitt. The occasion was the post-race function held at a spectacular outdoor venue, right under the Great Wall, lit up for the occasion and towering over proceedings. Everyone was in a joyous mood, especially Laurent. He was seated next to Andrea and had introduced himself to me in his heavily accented English, and with a mischievous full-faced grin. I wondered: 'Who does he think he is, this tall, handsome Frenchman flirting so openly with Andrea?' In no time, he had Andrea seated on his lap, his arms firmly wrapped around her as if to protect her from the evening chill, all the while chirping in her ear. Andrea seemed to be enjoying whatever Laurent was saying, oblivious to the stern looks from her coach.

I felt some responsibility for her wellbeing. This kind of distraction is not good for an athlete's career and doesn't do much for a coach's mood. But I needn't have worried. Laurent came to New Zealand that summer and respected me as Andrea's coach, and Andrea, level-headed as she is, got on with the business of training. After all, it was the year of the Beijing Olympics – where Andrea finished 8th and Laurent 36th, indicating that perhaps Laurent was the one who had been distracted.

When I took a break from coaching after Beijing, Laurent decided he would take over my role as Andrea's coach, much against my advice. Generally, it doesn't work if your coach is the same person you share your bed with. But Laurent and Andrea proved me wrong. Andrea not only kept up her consistent performances but she kept improving. They knew how to separate their personal relationship from that of coach–athlete, and they made it work. Under Laurent's guidance, Andrea finished 3rd in the World Championship Series in 2009, 2012 and 2014, and 2nd in 2011 and 2015.

During the time when I was coaching the Dutch team, the three of us often met on the international circuit. Laurent was full of ideas, questions, jokes and opinions, always the centre of attention. That suited Andrea, they complemented each other, and were clearly in love and very happy together.

At the London Olympics in 2012 Laurent finished 5th and Andrea 6th. A year later Laurent started to suffer from unexplained dizzy spells when racing. In April 2014 he suffered a cardiac arrest while training in the swimming pool in his hometown of Sète in Southern France. He had to retire from competition and decided to focus on coaching. Andrea and Laurent had planned to get married after the Rio 2016 Olympic Games; they had set the date and booked the venue.

On the evening of 10 November 2015 Andrea called me from Sète to tell me that Laurent had died suddenly in his sleep. He had suffered another cardiac arrest.

The funeral was in Sète, where Andrea and Laurent were based at the time. It was a solemn, heart-wrenching service without the anecdotes or laughter you sometimes get at funerals, but Laurent had died too suddenly, too unexpectly and too young for any of that. Andrea was in a state of grief-stricken disbelief.

The Rio Olympics were 10 months away and Andrea had just started the first week of her build-up when Laurent died. He would have wanted Andrea to get on with her life and that's what she had to do, with the Olympics her main target. But one week into her Olympic build-up, Andrea's campaign was in disarray. It had lost its most important driver, her coach, lover, constant companion and best friend. She needed support. Their close friend Kris Gemmel very quickly became the orchestrator of that support and helped her with the decisions and complexities left in the wake of Laurent's sudden departure.

Kris set to work and spent hours talking with Andrea to find out what she wanted, which was what Laurent had wanted. Together they scrolled through pages of documents on Laurent's computer to collect information that could be helpful, including provisional planning documents and training programmes.

And they decided on the most appropriate support team to help get her campaign back on track. Chris Pilone, friend of Laurent and coach of Olympic Gold medalist Hamish Carter, was appointed lead coach. Andrea's brother-in-law Nigel Cox had been Andrea's manager when I was coaching her and he took up that role again. My own role as an advisor was less defined, but Nigel called me kaumātua.[8] He must have felt I had some wisdom to pass on.

Kris led the group in the initial stages firmly and with a clear vision. He had obviously learned from life's experiences, as something in him had changed. He spoke in fewer riddles. He showed he had matured and that despite his intense grief, he knew what needed to be done. It was a proud moment for me as his former coach when I realised how far he had come.

After having stomach issues during the race, Andrea finished 7th at the Rio Olympics. Anybody with a heart would have wished for her to win a medal, but it was not to be. Competitive sport doesn't work like that.[9]

Laurent was passionate about keeping young athletes in triathlon, which can be an expensive sport. Inspired by Laurent, Andrea has established the AH Foundation to raise funds to support young and struggling triathletes in their quest for success.[10]

>>>

The women's race over, it was now up to the men. I had managed to obtain two tickets for the grandstand. By chance, Renzie Hanham, friend and mentor, was in Beijing for a conference. I invited him along, as I couldn't think of anyone better to share the experience with, whatever the outcome. Renzie turned up with a hangover the size of an elephant. He didn't have much to say, which was a good thing, as what unfolded was too cruel for words. It's only now, many years after the event, that I can commit the words to paper.

The race didn't start well for Kris. He missed the first bike after the swim, which was unlike him. He had to chase with some other stragglers for a few laps, which can take it out of your legs for the run. My emotions swung between hope and despair, but that was nothing new for me. Some coaches love watching the racing from the sideline. I don't. I feel helpless and frustrated, having no control over what happens out on the battlefield. Whenever possible, the day before or after a main event I would take part in the age-group race, trying to work off my emotional energy and calm my aggravated state of being. There is no age-group race at the Olympics.

Kris's group closed the gap to a large first bunch, a short reprieve for the coach. Hope. He was first off the bike into the transition and came out with a 20m lead to start the run. Could it be?

Renzie had fallen asleep beside me and didn't look well. Kris disappeared around a corner and up a small hill. I would have to wait about eight minutes for him to reappear to start his second of four laps. The time passed so slowly that I could have done a thousand things, but I just sat there listening to my fading heartbeat and thinking random unhelpful thoughts such as, if time heals all wounds, was this eternity a good thing for Kris's foot?

The first runners appeared. There was no Kris. A few more came by. I had counted 13 when he finally appeared. I was puzzled. 'Surely he could have gone full bore for at least one lap?' It was clear he had lost his mojo – he was head down, lumbering along. Did I see a limp? By the next lap he had drifted back even further. Despair. Renzie woke up and asked where he was. I gave him a dark look: 'In hell.'

We watched the remainder of the race in silence. I was oblivious to Jan Frodeno's spectacular victory and Bevan's podium finish.

Instead, I was with Kris, every agonising step of the way, urging him along: 'Finish, you bastard, at least finish.' That he did.

I met him at the finish line. He was beyond inconsolable and could not speak. We sat in silence for a while, then he started to talk. He had felt good, was not too worried about the swim. On the bike, he missed the first bunch, but did not panic as he knew they would catch up. 'Transition onto the run was great and I felt good. Then, on the first small hill I felt the insole of my shoe come loose and gradually curl up under my forefoot. I had to stop and take it out, then the same happened with the other insole during the second lap and I had to stop again. From then on I slip-slopped my way to the finish in shoes wet from water and sweat and two sizes too big without the insoles.' As he was talking, he was pulling hard on the skin of the still-healing wound on his foot, like he was possessed. I told him to stop. He carried on as if he hadn't heard, the wound started to bleed and I had to physically force his hand away from his foot.

The evening before the race Kris had the choice between two pairs of racing flats, his usual ones that did not have an insole, or an alternative pair that did. He sensibly chose the ones with the insoles to provide his injured foot with a bit more cushioning. A combination of heat, moisture and friction dislodged the poorly glued insole and that was that. I lay awake that night with thoughts about what might have been. It must have been a hundred times worse for Kris.

After the Olympics, Kris returned to Saarbrücken, where he shared a house with none other than gold medalist Jan Frodeno. He didn't respond to emails or phone calls. Finally, I got hold of him: he had been on the couch for two weeks, paralysed by despair. He was in a dark place.

Eventually he got up and going again. He had no choice, as triathlon was the only thing he knew. After the Beijing Olympics I stuck to my plan to have a break from front-line coaching and returned to my sports-medicine practice, though I also took on a part-time coach mentoring role with High Peformance Sport New Zealand. With mutual agreement I passed Kris on to Chris Pilone, who had coached Hamish to gold at the Athens Olympics. Under his guidance, Kris had four more years of competition at the highest level, and finished his career in 2012 with a credible 15th placing at the London Olympics.

CHAPTER 6

GOING DUTCH

Return to the motherland

Early in 2010, I received a telephone call from Adrie Berk, technical director for the Netherlands Triathlon Bond (NTB). I had met Adrie on occasion, at international events. This was not often, as Holland had few athletes of international repute at the time. After Eric van der Linden, Wieke Hoogzaad and the legendary Rob Barel, all prominent in the 1990s, the talent had dried up. Adrie explained that they wanted to close the gap with the international triathlon elite and they were looking for a coach with international experience to help them. Was I interested?

I had not considered a return to front-line coaching. I heard Adrie out, but my answer was, 'Thanks, but no thanks.' Immediately after I had put the phone down, however, I regretted my decision.

Adrie had explained that they had established a centralised programme a couple of years earlier, but the concept was not working well and they were in need of someone with experience to pull it together. A centralised programme was what I had had in mind when, in 1996, with the help of Terry Sheldrake and Graham

Park, I set up the New Zealand Triathlon Academy, in preparation for the Sydney Olympic Games. I'd had a clear vision of athletes and expertise being centralised in one region and Christchurch had been my choice, not because I lived there but because of its dry climate, ideal training terrain and good facilities.

But at that time New Zealand high performance sport wasn't ready for such a daring move. Also, the sport's power base was in the North Island, where the majority of athletes as well as the administration were based. The New Zealand Triathlon High Performance Programme, as it is now known, became a de-centralised programme supporting athletes and their coaches in the major regions. Now I had been offered a chance to head a centralised programme, a model I believed in but had been unable to achieve in New Zealand – and I'd turned it down. For a while my regret became all-consuming and I nearly called Adrie back to tell him I had changed my mind.

The intensity of my disappointment took me by surprise. It meant there was still a flame burning deep inside. Unfinished business? There always is for a coach. A search for adventure? Not likely; I could think of better adventures. A return to the motherland? Perhaps. Or was it just that I'd given away an opportunity to lead a centralised programme, a model I strongly believed in?

A few weeks later, Adrie called again. My heart jumped, but he merely wanted to know if I was prepared to go through the list of applicants for the head coach position. They'd had a lot of interest from overseas coaches and surely I would know most of them. I did, although not very well, but I didn't tell Adrie that.

There were a couple of Aussies, a coach from Luxembourg, one from Canada and a few others. When I saw the list of names I decided instantly that none of them could possibly do the job. I told

Adrie so, and heard myself saying I could be available if he gave me a bit of time to confer with Ien and tidy up my affairs in New Zealand. My only condition was that the athletes must come to New Zealand in our summer so I could show them how it's done in this sports-mad country. Since Adrie had already counted on training camps in New Zealand, the deal was done.

An added incentive was that during my tenure as head coach of the Dutch Triathlon Team I would be able to spend a bit of time with my mother who was by then 90 years old, and still living independently in her house on the shores of Lake Paterswolde. While the training programme was based at the opposite end of the country, 300km south of where she lived, that didn't seem too far to me; I was used to travelling much greater distances in New Zealand. I signed the contract with Dutch Triathlon in early July 2010, but my mother passed away suddenly two weeks later, before I had a chance to see her.

>>>

After 35 years as an expat in New Zealand, my re-entry into the Dutch culture – an eclectic mix of conservative Calvinism and exuberant liberalism – was both amusing and frustrating. Traditions and rituals that have developed over hundreds of years are strongly ingrained in the daily lives of the Dutch, even if they have been challenged in recent years by an influx of thousands of immigrants with a rich mix of cultural backgrounds. To the outsider that I now was, there appeared to be an excess of social control accompanied by a bewildering set of rules and regulations, but initially I was accorded foreigner status and excused for cutting corners and doing things differently. I got a whole lot done.

The privileges that come with a welfare state had created a culture of entitlement that has become part of the Dutch psyche. One of my goals as head coach was to change the athletes' mindset. I noticed everything was organised for them and they were very well looked after. That is not a good starting point for an athletic career: you should have no rights or privileges unless you perform.

The Dutch have a strong sense of social equality. This is admirable in principle, but in practice – especially in combination with that sense of entitlement – it translates into wanting to get the same as everyone else, regardless of effort. For an athlete, keeping an eye on what other athletes are getting is an unnecessary distraction. In addition, high performance sport in the Netherlands is still held back by a feeling – part of the national psyche – that it's best to fit in and not stand out (hence the oft-used expression *doe maar gewoon*, 'just be normal'), thereby denying diversity and excellence. This is in stark contrast with the liberal side of Dutch culture, in the arts and politics, for example, where tolerance rules. To change the mindset of entitlement to one of self-reliance and toughness seemed a first requirement for success. I explained to the athletes, coaches and support personnel how a culture of hard work and no expectations would best prepare them for international competition.

The strength of Dutch high performance sport lies in its organisational structure (it is club-based) and attention to technique. The Dutch excel in technical sports like soccer, hockey, sailing, swimming and ice speed-skating. My plan was to marry that structure and attention to technical detail with the passion and toughness of the Kiwis. Surely, I thought, world beaters would come out the other end.

>>>

The Dutch National Triathlon Training Centre is based in Sittard in Limburg, the southernmost province of the Netherlands, unfamiliar to me because I grew up in the far north. The landscape is different from the rest of Holland – gentle rolling hills of farmland, heaths, forests and quaint villages dominate the horizon – and even the architecture is not the same. Limburg is one of the most popular cycling provinces of Europe, with an unbelievable choice of bike paths and routes. It also has its own microclimate – warmer, sunnier, less windy and dryer than the rest of the country. Perhaps that's why the locals are more cheerful and laid-back than their counterparts in the flatter and wetter parts of the country. So the setting, at least, was idyllic.

The Olympic squad would ultimately consist of five mostly young and inexperienced Dutch women, Danne Boterenbrood, Sarissa de Vries, Neiske Becks, Maaike Caelers and Rachel Klamer, plus two imported athletes, Lisa Mensink from Canada and the only male, Jan van Berkel from Switzerland. These two had Dutch passports and Dutch names, but that's where their Dutchness stopped. Lisa Mensink was an experienced athlete who had already represented the Netherlands at the 2008 Beijing Olympics. She had not been able to achieve selection in her home country. On paper, she was an obvious asset to the team. Jan van Berkel had a Dutch father and therefore the passport. Like Lisa, he was also not on the Olympic selection radar in his own country, so he knocked on the Dutch door. To my bewilderment and frustration, top Dutch male triathletes avoided the ITU circuit, instead choosing the safety and guaranteed success of the Dutch triathlon circuit. There was one exception. We did have one promising male athlete from Holland in the training squad initially, Youri Severin, but he did not last long.

My goal to change the mindset of the athletes from entitlement to self-reliance depended to some extent on developing harmonious relationships within the team. I was aware of the fact that women in high performance sport can have difficulty living, training and competing in close proximity for long periods of time. What's more, as I noted earlier, it's hard to build a team culture in triathlon; individual athletes in the same squad have to compete against each other, which encourages feelings of jealousy, envy and distrust. This competition inevitably poses a threat to social harmony, which I have found to be more important for female athletes than it is for their male counterparts;[1] males tend to put the task at hand – training, competing and winning – ahead of relationships with their colleagues. What I hadn't counted on was the already dysfunctional nature of the relationships between the women in our squad, which was amplified by the centralised nature of the programme.

Disturbance and disruption

We had our first training camp in New Zealand during the early months of 2011, high summer in this part of the world. It was in the early days of my tenure and I was still getting to know the athletes. The camp was attended by Lisa, Rachel, Sarissa, Neiske, Maaike and Youri, who shared a large house in Christchurch. Jan van Berkel had not yet joined the squad and Danne Boterenbrood had study committments.

Three separate incidents occurred in quick succession during the first two weeks of the camp, and to a large degree they were to define my next three years with the Dutch programme.

Within a few days the dysfunctional relationships between the women came to the surface, magnified by the close living arrangements. I sensed an unhappiness within the group, manifested in sly remarks, derogatory comments, loaded questions, silent stares, factions within the wider group and overzealous competitive behaviour during training sessions. Perhaps individually these behaviours might not have been too destructive, but thrown together in the melting pot of the training camp and boiled for long enough, they resulted in a toxic mix.

The first incident involved Youri Severin. Towards the end of the first week he had an argument with one of the female athletes. He lost his temper and slapped her in the face and when another of the women tried to intervene he pushed her hard against a cupboard. Neither of them wanted to involve the police, but this behaviour demanded a clear and unambiguous response: violence would not be tolerated. I had no choice but to send Youri back home to Holland, where he was disciplined by the Netherlands Triathlon Bond. It was one of the darker moments of my coaching career.

Soon after that first incident one of the athletes woke up one morning to discover too late that detergent had been added to the solution in which she stored her contact lenses overnight. The pain was excruciating. This was an insidious act of violence, with an element of psychological bullying; there were no witnesses and no one owned up. Short of sending everyone home, it was difficult to know what to do. I planned to focus on team dynamics over the next three weeks during our altitude training camp.

The following day we travelled to the Snow Farm lodge high in the mountains between the tourist resorts of Wanaka and Queenstown. On the second day of the altitude camp, however, my plans were shaken up by news of the third event: Christchurch had been hit by an earthquake measuring 6.3 on the Richter scale.

Racing back to a city in ruins

It is 12.51pm on 22 February 2011. The Dutch triathlon team have come down from their altitude base at Snow Farm for a swim training session in the Queenstown pool. It is a 45-minute journey and we have just arrived when my mobile phone rings. It's Ien. Her voice is shaking. There has been an earthquake. I can hear rumbling sounds in the background. Ien's panicky response makes me realise they are aftershocks. 'Ien, are you okay?' The phone goes dead. 'Ien, are you okay?'

I'm overcome by waves of worry and guilt. I was away when the magnitude 7.1 earthquake struck Canterbury in September the previous year, so Ien had to fend for herself then, too. I was on the other end of the phone, even further away in Holland, mopping up after the competitive season and preparing for the next. Ien and our house came out of that first big earthquake unscathed. It struck in the early hours of a Sunday morning, and while there was significant damage across the city, no lives were lost. This time it sounds more serious. Ien comes back on the line. She's crying. The whole house moved up and down, she tells me. She was standing in the doorway and had to hold on with both hands to stop herself from falling.

'I'm coming home,' I say. At least this time I'll be able to see her within a few hours. Another loud noise comes through the phone, followed by a shriek. 'Ien, are you there? Ien … ?' Silence, apart from a crackle from the phone. Thinking the worst, I panic, but then she's back on the line again. She is unable to string proper sentences together, words tumble randomly out of her mouth. 'Broken glass everywhere' and 'food all over the floor' and 'big mess'. Suddenly she announces that she has to go. Minutes later my phone rings again and she tells me she is okay. She's met neighbours on the turning bay at the end of our driveway, and they've found solace in each other's company. My urge to be there with her is overwhelming.

I have my bike in the van, as I was planning to ride back in the direction of Snow Farm after the swim session, when the team want to have a look around Queenstown. I tell swim coach Roly Crichton I'm leaving them in his hands and hop on my bike to head back to our accommodation, where my car is. Even though the team will make it back faster than me, it's the first step towards getting home and I want to be moving. The team will pick me up on their way back to the lodge.

The Snow Farm lodge is on a plateau 1600m above sea level, called the Pisa Range. Car and tyre manufacturers fly in from all over the world to test their new inventions and equipment on the winter roads before the start of the Northern Hemisphere winter season.

The distance from Queenstown is 58km, but they are no ordinary kilometres. They include the notorious Crown Range, the highest sealed pass in New Zealand, reaching an altitude of 1121m. Coming from Queenstown, you climb over a distance of 11km with an average gradient of 10–11%. A fast descent on the other side brings you into the Cardrona Valley and halfway up the valley a private, unsealed road winds up the Pisa Range for 13km, with an 11–12% gradient. The loose and rutted surface makes it unsuitable for a road bike, but I calculate the team van will catch up with me well before the turn-off.

I calm down as soon as I hop on my bike. The overwhelming sense of helplessness and worry evaporates; Ien is safe and I'm on my way home. That's better than standing around at the pool, fretting. The afternoon is sunny and tranquil when I set out. Soon

I'm climbing up the familiar zig-zag of the Crown Range. The climb is a key component of the training during the camps we've had over the years and I'm climbing strongly, spurred on by my desire to get to my destination.

I've taken off in a hurry with minimal provisions or clothing, and by halfway up the climb temperatures have dropped to chilly. A nagging doubt enters my mind – have I made the right decision? Should I perhaps have taken the van to go straight to Christchurch and left Roly and the athletes to work out an alternative way to return to base after the swim?

I'm nearing the top of the climb and the air is getting closer to freezing with every metre of altitude gained. Dark clouds start to pour across the mountain tops from the other side, heralding a south-westerly change. This is not good. Early splatters turn to rain, then sleet. Despite the considerable physical effort that I'm putting into the climb, I start to shiver. The only thing I can do is to push on, as there is little traffic and nowhere to shelter.

By the time I hit the top of the pass, the storm unleashes all its fury. Until now I have been looking forward to the downhill, but not anymore. The ice-cold sleet hammers my face, bare legs and arms, like a nail gun gone berserk. My skin turns instantly turns pimply red, before it changes to dark blue and then thankfully goes numb. Despite the downhill gradient, the force of the wind slows me to a crawl.

I push on, certain that the van can't be far behind and will soon pick me up. But I arrive at the turnoff to Snow Farm, wet and chilled to the bone, and still there's no van. The weather hasn't improved and I have to keep moving to prevent hypothermia. I start to ride up the Snow Farm road to warm up from the descent, despite knowing full well how difficult it will be. The soft sand

and loose stones, mixed with the wet, have turned the road into a heavy slush. Stopping is not an option, as there is no way to get going again. I'm forced to commit. My body starts to warm up a little, but that doesn't last long because when I hit a bit of altitude the temperature drops below freezing and it starts to snow.

I look back, but still no van in sight. With the road getting steeper, my world narrows down to the sole purpose of staying upright. I have long since run out of food and drink and I feel my body weaken, slowing down with each revolution of the pedals. 'Keep turning those pedals, John, one stroke at the time. Whatever you do, don't stop.'

I resign myself to the fact that the van is not coming, that I'm on my own. The thought that people in Christchurch are faring much worse than me keeps me going. A little later, a white dot appears on the road far below. I keep biking to feed the flicker of warmth my labouring muscles have created. It takes the van another 20 minutes to reach me.

'Where the hell have you been?' I manage to blurt out as soon as they get to me.

The crisis in Christchurch is far enough away for them not to have fully grasped its impact, and they've been oblivious to the extent of my anxiety and the pressure I've put on myself to get home urgently. They look at me in shock when they see the state I'm in. Now that I've stopped moving, I'm shivering uncontrollably. The athletes pile out of the van, peel my frozen hands off the handlebars, lift me off the bike and help me into the van. They dry, dress and feed me. By the time we reach Snow Farm, I feel half-human again.

But I'm upset, since the whole ordeal on the bike has cost me valuable time, so after a hot bath and a quick meal, I hop into my car for the journey back to Christchurch. By this stage it's nearly 8pm. I have the company of a sports science student, who is doing research on altitude training with our group. She's also desperate to return to Christchurch to check on her mates.

I should be exhausted, but I'm not. I'm wired, amped up with a huge dose of nervous energy. I put my foot down as soon as we hit the open road, thinking that in this crisis I finally have a good excuse to put the Jaguar XJ through its paces – 140 ... 160... 180km/hr. ... it performs perfectly, a dream of a ride (as it should be, considering the small fortune it cost me); it's glued to the road and drifts through the bends at racing car speed. There are no cops about and little traffic. Dusk falls, soon shifting into darkness, but that doesn't slow us down.

In record time, we hit State Highway One at Ashburton, 90km south of Christchurch. There is a long line of cars queued up at the petrol station. Many are towing trailers loaded to the brim with goods and possessions. I line up and am desperate to get the latest information. The stories are grim. I am warned that it's a 'war zone', that I shouldn't venture there.

An ambulance is filling up and I recognise the medic. 'What's the story?' I ask her. She says she's not sure, they had been held up and should have been in Christchurch hours ago. So should I, goes through my mind. After filling up I get back into the car and drive away against the slow-moving dance of headlights; our side of the road is completely deserted except for the flashing lights of the ambulance ahead of us, rapidly disappearing into the distance.

Now I keep to a more respectable pace. When we reach Halswell, on the outskirts of Christchurch, the main sign that something is amiss is the absence of street lighting. It is also eerily quiet and the roads are deserted. When I get closer to the city centre I can see fires burning, lighting up the sky. We know from radio reports that the west of the city has been largely spared. That's where the sports science student lives, so I drop her off at her flat and head east in the direction of the fires.

The first real manifestation of the shaken earth is a huge sinkhole in the middle of the road – with the rear end of a car visible in the middle. I manoeuvre carefully around this first obstacle. The road is covered in a thick layer of heavy grey mud and I'm puzzled: 'Where the hell has that come from?' It's my first experience of liquefaction.[2]

There are more sinkholes randomly dispersed across the road, which becomes increasingly difficult to negotiate, with only my car headlights to show the way in the pitch-black darkness. Strange undulations and immense cracks in the road are further hazards. I come to a halt at the Ferrymead Bridge, a link across the Heathcote River between the city and the seaside suburb of Sumner, where we live. The bridge is blocked by a loose cordon of cones and yellow tape. A sign warns: 'Bridge unsafe, use detour.'

I get out of the car. The bridge has been lifted above road level and is sitting at an unnatural angle. It's covered by pieces of asphalt dislodged by the force of the quake. I get ready to grab my bike and carry it over on foot, but I don't want to leave my car amidst the chaos, even if there are plenty of other abandoned cars there. I decide to explore the detour, which goes over a piece of motorway that crosses the river further back. I get through somehow. The causeway – the road that runs along the estuary on the other side of the Ferrymead Bridge – is heavily damaged; there are large craters and cracks everywhere, as if it's been bombed.

There is one more potential obstacle to face. Our house is situated halfway up Clifton Hill, nearly 200m above sea level. The access road is precarious at the best of times, with sharp corners and steep inclines. I find it's now blocked by a sizeable rockfall with cars buried underneath. I get out, shift a few rocks, and squeeze my car through a small gap. Except for the cracks and bumps in the road and plenty of loose rocks, there is no more drama and I finally roll into our driveway at 2.30am. It has taken me nearly as long to get from one side of Christchurch to the other, a journey of 20km, as it took me to cover the 400km between Wanaka and Christchurch.

Ien hears me coming. She has been trying to sleep on the couch at the neighbour's house, but worry and aftershocks have kept her awake. It's a relief to wrap my arms around her and hold her close. I take a torch and survey the damage inside the house, which is filled with an overwhelming smell of dead fish courtesy of a bottle of fish sauce that has crashed out of the pantry. Except for large cracks in the walls the house looks structurally sound; built on poles, it has swayed with the movements of the earth. With help from the neighbour, Ien has cleaned up the worst of the mess, but with no water or electricity she's been limited in what she can do.

We decide to go to bed and deal with it all in the morning. Ien falls immediately into a deep sleep. Waiting for each new aftershock, I sit up straight in bed all night, like a stunned possum caught in the headlights of an oncoming car. The aftershocks announce themselves with a loud 'boom' or low rumble, followed by a violent shaking of the house, and rattling of doors, windows and blinds. I can't believe Ien is sleeping through the noise, but she's experienced much worse.

>>>

First light breaks and we're greeted by total silence; there's a noticeable absence of early morning birdsong. Every now and then the stillness is disturbed by thumping noises coming from the restless earth. Through a haze of smoke and dust, we look at the broken city skyline in the distance. There are gaps where buildings stood before, other buildings are leaning dangerously to one side, and columns of smoke indicate smouldering ruins. Closer to home, surveying the cliffs across the valley through binoculars, I can see that part of the cliff edge has given way and houses are dangling perilously over the edge, while others lie smashed to pieces at the foot of the cliff.

The first sign of life is the sound of helicopters whirring overhead. People start to venture onto the roads, some of them by car. The radio updates us on access roads and escape routes, water stations, emergency locations and numbers. There are more than 300 people missing. Among them is a good friend.

I call the emergency services and offer my medical expertise, but the one thing they have enough of is medical personnel. Emergency physicians and surgeons are flying in from the North Island and Australia and sports medicine doctors are not high on their wish list. After my offer of help is declined, I shift my attention to the house in New Brighton where the Dutch athletes – safely tucked away at Snow Farm – have their Christchurch base.

I go by mountain bike because the roads leading to the suburb of New Brighton are torn apart by cracks the size of crevasses, and the bridge across the Avon River has tilted off its pillars and is too dangerous to cross. I haul the bike onto my shoulder and climb across the bridge anyway; surely it can hold one person and a bike. On the other side is New Brighton, closed off from the rest of the world, and most of it knee-deep in water.

Once at the house, I realise how lucky the team was to be out of town when the quake hit. The house is still standing, but that's all that can be said. Inside, there isn't one piece of furniture standing in the right place. The same applies to the crockery, which is strewn in a thousand pieces over the kitchen floor. The walls are cracked in several places, with great chunks missing, and the fireplace has been ripped out of the wall. Most of the windows are completely blown out.

Aftershocks fill the rooms with dust as I go through the house. I have kept my bike helmet on, though I'm not sure how much good it will do if the house comes down. I call the athletes to find out what I should rescue from among their personal belongings. The one thing they all want is their race wheels, of course, as their first event is looming in a couple of weeks. I strap as many of them together as possible. With the wheels slung over my shoulder, I bike home with renewed purpose and direction.

I return the next day with Ien, travelling by car with a trailer in tow, a harrowing journey that takes us more than two hours instead of the usual 15 minutes. We suspect it's only a matter of time before looters arrive, hence the urgency. We stuff all the athletes' remaining gear into their bike boxes to take to Snow Farm.

On Sunday, five days after the earthquake and with mixed feelings of relief, sadness and guilt, we leave Christchurch for the Snow Farm. Halfway there, at Omarama, we get the dreaded news that there is no hope that our friend Lesley will be found alive. She was at an appointment in the destroyed CTV building, a place she had never visited before and was planning to be in for only 20 minutes.

Dazed by the news, I mistakenly fill the car with petrol rather than diesel. It's Sunday afternoon, but the petrol station owner comes from his home and works on my car for two hours to correct my mistake. He doesn't charge me; it feels as if the whole country is behind Christchurch. Every New Zealander knows someone who is affected in one way or another.

Picking up the pieces

As a consequence of the February 2011 earthquakes 185 people died, and many more were injured. The impact of the quakes on the natural and built environment was severe and long-lasting. Some 100km of sewerage and 50km of roading were severely damaged. The rivers were contaminated for some time with spilled sewage and wastewater. Many water stations and water pipes were out of action or damaged, causing a period of water shortages and polluted drinking water. Areas where land had subsided became prone to flooding. A total 30,000 tonnes of liquefaction silt had to be removed and six million tonnes of demolition rubble were dumped in a newly created landfill. Nine bridges were taken out of use until they could be repaired or rebuilt.

It was clear to us that we could not return to Christchurch after our altitude training camp at Snow Farm and so we based ourselves further north, in Nelson.

The team dynamics had not improved. Theoretically, the Dutch women's triathlon team possessed an ideal combination of skills and strengths: there were two strong swim/bike specialists, one senior and one junior all-rounder, and a couple of fast runners. They should have been able to help each other in training and during races but working together seemed to be the last thing on their minds. There was nothing I could do to stop the wrecking ball of female 'diplomacy' at work.

We involved psychologists and counsellors, had numerous team meetings, and asked the athletes themselves to set rules around expected behaviour. Everyone expressed the need for mutual respect, but words were meaningless as long as the athletes were trapped in a pattern of negative thoughts and feelings about each other. The eventual disintegration of the team following the intense qualifying period prior to the London Olympics became inevitable.

From the core group of six female athletes, only two turned out to be 100% committed to me as their coach. They were also the ones who won medals on the world stage during my time, although that could be coincidence. One of the athletes indicated that she wanted me to coach her 'for 90%'. 'Really? And which 90% would that be?' Another kept consulting her old coach. I didn't mind, except they were secretive about it. That doesn't work. Coaches working together is a powerful thing; if they don't, it's a sure recipe for disaster for the athlete.

My working relationship with a third athlete was good when we were away on training camps, but deteriorated quickly every time we returned to home base, when her father's influence took over. A fourth was frequently seen doing extra training.

But then, why should the athletes have trusted me unconditionally? They'd had this new coach thrust upon them, a stranger they had never heard of, who had deserted his country to live on the other side of the world, only to come back speaking with a funny accent.

I hadn't been prepared for this situation. Until then, it had been athletes who came to me to be coached. I had always been in the driver's seat. This time I had to earn the athletes' trust. That I never fully succeeded in doing this was as much due to failings on my part as it was to the interplay of their personalities and cirumstances.

One of the athletes was particularly vulnerable to the intricacies of team dynamics. In social groups that don't function well, it's the weakest link that gets picked on. It's no different in competitive sport. Sooner or later, athletes who don't stand up for themselves, regardless of their talent, are pushed out or give up. I decided to step in and protect the 'weakest' athlete as much as possible from the team dynamics, but in doing so I risked the perception of favouritism. It's considered a cardinal sin in coaching to express even the slightest hint of preferential treatment, but in this case compassion took precedence over my role as coach. The fact that the athlete showed promise and total commitment contributed to my decision to treat her as a special case.

Coaches are human, too. Consciously or subconsciously, they are likely to invest more in athletes who trust them 100% than in those who keep their options open. But favouritism, real or perceived, can be the knockout blow for team dynamics. Despite my efforts to act as inconspicuously as possible, my protective attitude towards the athlete was soon picked up by the others. They blamed the athlete, rather than me, so in the end my strategy had the reverse effect.

The 2012 London Olympics

By picking their ITU points races strategically, five of the six women achieved a ranking in the top 100 in the world in 2011. This made them eligible to start in the World Triathlon Series (WTS) Olympic qualifying races held in early 2012.

Jan van Berkel didn't join us until late 2011; he wasn't ranked in the top 100, but he was all we had. His start in the Olympic qualifying races depended on athletes from other countries pulling out. I risked taking him to New Zealand with the team early in 2012, as I felt he could potentially act as a distractor and buffer in the tricky female team dynamics. He had a law degree and combined with his amenable personality that made him as suitable for this role as anyone. He also trained like a demon and lived like a hermit in an attempt to get to the Olympics. A good role model, I thought. And who knows, there was always the outside chance he could 'do a Bradbury'.[3]

The first Olympic qualifier was the WTS race held in Sydney in April 2012. We returned to Nelson for three months to prepare. Neiske Becks was replaced by Danne Boterenbrood who had missed the 2011 camp. Our build-up was marred not only by unhappy team dynamics, but also by injury and illness. This was no surprise as research confirms that unhappiness can weaken the immune system and increase the chance of injury. The results were dismal, with Rachel Klamer achieving the highest placing at 25th while the rest lingered near the back of the field or withdrew. That was so far off the mark that I offered my resignation to Adrie Berk, who had flown over especially for the race. He wasn't going to let me off that easily, however, and refused to accept.

Based on our world rankings, we were in a position to have two female athletes on the start line at the Olympics. The maximum number per country is three. The Dutch Olympic Committee had set its own tough qualification criterion: in addition to a top-55 world ranking, the athletes needed a top-12 finish in any of the three designated qualifying WTS events. In the unlikely event that more than two women achieved this a complicated points system would decide final selection.

In 2011, three of the women had achieved 8th, 10th and 11th placings in three out of seven similar races, so we knew it could be done. But in Olympic year the fields are always stronger because everyone is stepping up their efforts in the chase for that elusive Olympic berth. We had improved, but so had everyone else. A top-12 in a WTS event in that Olympic year was going to be a huge task for our mostly inexperienced team.

After the Sydney disaster, the senior athlete in the team, Dutch-Canadian Lisa Mensink, had had enough of the team dynamics and requested a release so she could prepare in the familiar surroundings of her home country for the crucial second and third Olympic qualifying events. I could not blame her.

Danne Boterenbrood, who had placed 8th at the Hamburg leg of the WTS the previous year, had gone into the Sydney race sick and was forced to withdraw. She went home to Holland to recuperate and put all her eggs in the basket of the third qualifying race held in Madrid in late May. She didn't have much choice, because the rest of us were off to altitude in North America to prepare for the second race in San Diego. As mentioned previously, altitude and illness don't go together well.

Flagstaff and Sedona in Northern Arizona were carefully chosen for our preparation for the San Diego race. It allowed us to divide up the squad, with the more resilient athletes, Jan van Berkel and Sarissa de Vries, based at Flagstaff at 1800m, accompanied by swim coach Jordi Meulenberg. The two youngest athletes, Maaike Caelers and Rachel Klamer, were housed with me at the safer altitude of 1200m in Sedona, one hour by car from Flagstaff.

To give an athlete an edge, my coaching philosophy has always been to try to get the basis of training, nutrition and mental attitude right first and then add something special, a new training technique or a challenging environment, like altitude. Training in the rarefied air of the mountains provides additional stress, and consequently favourable adaptations in the body in relation to the oxygen-processing mechanisms. On return to sea level, the adaptations come in handy as the body gets a temporary boost when suddenly exposed to a relatively oxygen-rich environment.

In our case, we didn't really have the basics right; training had been interrupted and the mental state of the athletes, with the exception of Jan van Berkel, was fragile to say the least. But the plans had been made well in advance and the challenge was to make it work as best we could.

The race in San Diego was the best chance for our athletes to qualify, as some of the stronger European nations were staying home to concentrate on the WTS event in Madrid two weeks later. With Danne still recuperating in Holland, Rachel, Maaike, Sarissa, Lisa and Jan toed the starting line in San Diego. The weather conditions were calm and sunny, the pleasant temperatures contrasting with the tension, which was palpable. For the Americans on home soil, this was their final selection event. All eyes were on them. Could we benefit from that?

Our women didn't have the best of starts. During the swim, a group of nine athletes opened a distinct gap on the rest of the field. Rachel hung on the tail of this group in last position. She lost contact through a slow transition and saw the remaining eight athletes disappear into the distance. As a coach, you can explain potential situations to athletes till the cows come home, but often they have to experience something first-hand before they really understand; it's a painful but effective way to learn. When you're in the back of a group, rather than thinking: 'I'm with the group, great,' your focus needs to be on not losing them. A fast transition is crucial.

The group of eight included Americans Laura Bennett and Sarah Haskins, as well as Helen Jenkins (Great Britain) and Erin Densham (Australia). They weren't going to wait for anyone and worked well together to try to increase the gap on a large, disorganised pursuing bunch.

When Rachel came past after the first of eight laps, she was still caught in no-man's-land between the two groups. I instructed her to wait for the second bunch, which would invariably catch her anyway. That group contained the remaining Dutch athletes, Lisa, Sarissa and Maaike, the latter the best runner. She'd had a semi-decent swim, her weak discipline, and had made use of the erratic pace of the bunch to catch up quickly. I thought all was not lost.

Then, disaster. Restlessness at the front of the group, with athletes trying to avoid the lead position, resulted in a crash after they bunched up too much going around a narrow bend. It happened close to the transition area where I was positioned. The noise of screeching brakes was followed by the sickening sound of bikes and bodies colliding with one another and slamming into the unforgiving asphalt.

Lisa was involved. She quickly scrambled back to her feet ready to remount her bike, only to be mowed down by a rider behind who was unable to avoid her. This time she did not get up – her elbow was shattered in two places. Our most experienced athlete was out. The remaining three had avoided the carnage.

Meanwhile, the eight women at the front of the race built an insurmountable lead of more than two minutes. That meant, to achieve a top-12 finish, our three women had to be among the four fastest runners from their large group of more than 30 riders.

Rachel and Maaike ran close together in places 14 and 15 for the first couple of laps. Not good enough. Sarissa drifted back through the field and out of contention. In the third lap, Maaike and Rachel had worked themselves up to places 11 and 12. The adaptations to altitude started to kick in and the race for our two qualifying spots was on.

But Maaike had copped a 15-second stand-down penalty when she omitted to put her swim cap in her designated box during the swim-to-bike transition. The race numbers of athletes with penalties are written for all to see on a whiteboard at the start of the run. The stand-down time can be taken in an area called the penalty box at any point during the run.

'Take it after the third lap,' I shouted at her during the first of four running laps.

'I don't want to,' she shot back at me.

At the end of the third lap she had come to her senses and stopped to take her 15 seconds. She was still running in 11th position at that stage, with Rachel Klamer hard on her heels in 12th. A placing in the top 12 would earn them nomination for a place at the start line of the London Olympic Triathlon.

I was standing next to the penalty box to make sure Maaike kept it together. The referee was waiting for her to come to a complete standstill before he pressed his stopwatch. Maaike immediately challenged him and told him in no uncertain terms to start his watch. Instead, he looked at her with disdain, deliberately stalling and telling her to calm down first, which wound her up even more. 'The bastard,' I thought. 'He's making up his own rules.' But we had to go with it and I yelled at her in Dutch to shut up.

Rachel and Maaike were closely pursued by a silent line of competitors in varying degrees of distress. The final 3km of a World Series race are murderous, because every place counts for Olympic and world rankings, as well as prize money. The tank is empty and the body screams at you to slow down, but there's no time to take the foot off the gas and think, 'Oh well, I'm not going to win today. I'm going to save myself for the next race.'

When Maaike re-joined the race, she had dropped back to 16th; that's how tight the racing was. Five women had come past within the 15-plus seconds of the penalty. Was she going to run out of road? But in her fury she quickly overtook the athletes who had passed her, including her team-mate. Relief – Maaike and Rachel took 11th and 12th respectively; two berths, and two qualifiers.

In the men's race, Jan van Berkel, who had put so much into his preparation, was never in contention. His engine was simply not big enough. He realised this and, although he was still on the waiting list for a start in Madrid, he decided to quit his Olympic campaign. No more for him.

It was still possible for Danne and Sarissa to steal the two Olympic spots from Maaike and Rachel if they finished in the top 10 and ahead of their team-mates in Madrid two weeks later. But Danne had run out of time to regain full fitness and went under fighting, finishing 33rd. Sarissa was plagued by exercise-induced asthma even before the race started. Madrid has one of the most allergenic conditions of all races on the circuit, and every year dozens of athletes succumb to the devastating effect of constricted airways that have been exposed to air thick with pollen and related allergens. Maaike suffered the same fate. She had collapsed in the race the previous year, unable to breathe, and this time she struggled to the finish line as one of the last competitors, in 54th spot.

Freed from the shackles of still having to make the qualifying criteria and knowing she would have the better of any of the others, Rachel had the race of her life, finishing in a personal-best 5th position. For three months, she had carried a stress fracture of her shin bone. Getting 12th and 5th in two out of three qualifying races meant she deserved her Olympic spot.

An anxious wait followed the race. Maaike's poor result meant the second Olympic starting slot for Holland was under threat. But at 11 o'clock that night we got a phone call confirming our two qualifying spots. If Austria had finished 16th instead of 17th, they would have overtaken us for that second berth. Rachel and Maaike were off to their first Olympics.

>>>

We had three months to recover from the brutal qualifying period and prepare for the biggest sporting event in the universe. It was not enough. The girls were exhausted and so was the coach. The two athletes were the youngest, least experienced and least compatible of the group, and I was torn in half for three months trying to make it work. The results in London, in front of millions of viewers, were forgettable 36th and 41st placings.

Rachel joined the Olympic after-party, but Maaike was not happy and requested a training programme to start the day after the race. In the following months, she became the first Dutch athlete to score WTS podiums, by coming 2nd at the WTS in Stockholm (a race that doubled as the World Sprint Championships) and 3rd in Yokohama soon after.

>>>

Rachel Klamer has carved out a solid career on the ITU circuit and finished 10th at the Rio Olympic Games. In 2018 she had her first win in a WTS event in Abu Dhabi. Maaike has raced only intermittently in the last couple of years due to health issues. She missed Rio but in 2017 came back as a member of the Dutch mixed-relay team, which, to everyone's surprise, won a bronze medal at the world championships in Hamburg.

A year after the London Olympics, Danne Boterenbrood swapped her Olympic dream for a stethoscope and resumed her medical career. Sarissa de Vries finished 2012 with a silver medal in the under-23 world championships in Auckland. She has since stepped up successfully to the longer distances. Lisa Mensink and Jan van Berkel cut ties with the Dutch programme after the London Games to pursue glory under the colours of their respective home countries, also in longer distance events.

I stayed on for another year after the London Olympics, but the team dynamics, the fallout from the Christchurch earthquakes, the travel and too much time away from my family had all taken a toll. I needed to let go. After three years, despite the difficulties, there was a solid programme in place. My job was done. When the athletes trained in New Zealand and mixed with Kiwi athletes they seemed to get it – the passion, toughness, hard work and resilience required – but every time we returned to Holland they regressed to their old habits and patterns. I'd felt the same transition happen within myself when I was there: I'd started to take holidays and cut my working hours down to nine-to-five where possible. All well and good in terms of fitting in, but it meant that I became part of the furniture and a less effective coach. It was time to say goodbye to the Dutch ways, though I would miss the wry humour and openness.

CHAPTER 7

THE CHALLENGE OF STAYING UPRIGHT

Hawaii, the ultimate test

It's Hawaii, 12 October 2013, and I come to a halt just before the infamous Palani Hill on my return to Kailua-Kona. It's 4km from the finish. I've swum 3.8km, biked 180km and run 38km – and the world has started to spin.

I must sit down before I keel over, I think, through the fog that invades my brain. I stagger. The world spins faster. I stop in the middle of the road, legs planted wide apart so I don't fall. The urge to let that happen, and to finally have an excuse to lie down, becomes overwhelming. *Shit, I'm not going to make it*, goes through my mind. An ambulance comes past, sirens blaring. It goes in the opposite direction to pick up some poor bastard. I'll be next. *I'll have to come back next year and do it all over again.* That thought gets me walking. The misery of staying upright wins over the misery of pulling out. The dizziness subsides somewhat, but my legs don't respond to my commands. 'Run, you pricks, run.' But they're not home.

>>>

I was in this mess thanks to Chipollini, who had told me a few years earlier that you're not a real triathlete till you've done the Hawaii Ironman. This Chipollini is fellow triathlete Neil Sheerin, nicknamed after Mario Chipollini, the flamboyant Italian cyclist best known for his devastating sprint. At the end of a group training ride once, Neil won a hotly contested sprint. Kris Gemmell, usually the winner of such informal competitions, pointed his finger at Neil and yelled out: 'Chipollini!' The name stuck.

I had shrugged my shoulders at Neil's suggestion. I'd done my one and only ironman in 2004 – it was the Almere Ironman Triathlon in Holland, the same race where Erin Baker started her international career in 1985. As expected, the suffering far exceeded the euphoria. The problem with the ironman is that during the first part of the event you worry about what's still to come, and in the later stages you find out you were right to worry. My experience then had left me none the wiser about why so many triathletes make it their event of choice, and I had no intentions of doing another one. My favourite distance has always been the standard or Olympic distance, a 1500m swim, 40km bike ride, and a 10km run. Red-line it for a couple of hours, go home, have a beer and a lie down.

However, Neil's challenge had got to me and it bothered me like a persistent toothache. 'Never,' I told it. 'Go away.' But it didn't. His words kept coming back, nag-nag-nag at the back of my mind: 'You're not a true triathlete till you've done Hawaii.' That's how I'd found myself at the starting line of the mother of all triathlons at the ripe old age of 60.

I had prepared as well as I could. I forced my ageing body through long training sessions to the point where my aching frame and deep-rooted tiredness became a permanent state. Normally, the body adapts and starts to feel better and stronger with continued training. But at 60, it doesn't adapt any more. You have to make do with what you've got, which ain't much.

The aching and fatigue got worse. I persevered. In the weeks prior to the race, I took a sauna three times a week to prepare for the heat and humidity I was going to be exposed to. All that did was add to my already interminable fatigue.

Just before the start of the race, next to the transition area, a familiar voice had broken through the nervous hum of thousands of competitors making last-minute preparations. It was Mark Allen who had called out to me, obviously surprised to see me at the startline. Mark was considered the Zen-master of triathlon, on account of his unflappable demeanour and tendency to spirituality. The last time I had seen him was in 1989 in Christchurch, where he had come to train for the summer with Scott Molina and Rob Barel. He had borrowed my broken-down Morris Minor for transport. It wasn't really roadworthy, but with Mark calmly behind the wheel it purred like an old tabby cat and never skipped a beat.

He was obviously surprised to see me. We shook hands. Mark still had the refined features of a greyhound, but his face was marked by age and too much sun. 'I finally made it,' I joked. 'I've trained for this day for 60 years.' He didn't reply, just smiled his Zen-like smile and nodded. He knew this race better than anyone. After all, he had failed six times before conquering the event and winning it as many times. He knew much better than me what I was in for.

And now I was finding out. I felt the energy ooze out of my body around 140km into the bike leg. I still had 40km to go before I could start the marathon run. The sun was beating down, it was 35°C, and Kona's unrelenting trade winds were torturing me. I was paying the price for an over-exuberant pace earlier on. Against better judgement, my competitiveness had taken over, and I hadn't wanted to drop out of the fast-moving bike pack on the way out to the turnaround point at Hawaii.

On the return journey, the large pack slowly disintegrated, beaten apart by the hot, swirling headwinds coming from the barren lava fields all around us. We each continued solo, affected to varying degrees by the demons that invariably arrive in all sorts of guises after four or five hours of racing. Overheating, dehydration and a sore bottom, back and shoulders are the main ones. I suffered all of those.

Then the 'bonk' hit – the moment when blood sugar drops below the critical level needed to feed working muscles. There are no warning signs; in a split-second I felt weak and lost all power. But it was not only my muscles that turned to jelly. Glucose is an essential fuel for brain function, so I couldn't think clearly. I slowed down. I had no say over it. The only thing I could do was eat, drink and preserve as much energy as possible to reverse the energy deficit that had forced my body into survival mode.

I wanted to stop and get off my bike, to lie down in the shade, but there was no shade anywhere in sight. A staunch-looking competitor came past and I jumped onto his wheel. Drafting out of the wind close behind another competitor saves you 30% in expended energy. That makes bike racing so unfair, frustrating, unpredictable and therefore exciting.

But this was not a bike race, and drafting isn't permitted in ironman triathlon. I was supposed to keep a respectable distance – 10m – but for a short time, I was happy to risk the customary four-minute penalty handed out randomly by the many draft busters. When I felt a bit better I dropped back. Despite that, 3km before the transition, a smug-looking referee waved a blue card at me from the pillion seat of a motorbike, indicating a penalty for drafting. It was long after I had left the drafting zone and I still wonder today where he got his intelligence. But I figured my enforced rest would do me good, and I was also in urgent need of a pee. Ever tried peeing while riding a bike? Well, I tell you, it ain't easy. I was going to make the most of the short break.

I arrived at the penalty box located inside the transition area and couldn't see a toilet. I was ready to let go. At that same moment, an angry-looking referee came up to me, his eyes glaring behind an enormous pair of spectacles, and through his heavy beard he hissed at me that if I pissed in his tent I would be disqualified. It was evident from the smell that others had done it before me and he'd had enough.

Other competitors in the same predicament looked away sheepishly. I was desperate and squirted my bladder contents out in minute amounts, trying to hide what I was doing by pouring water over my body, trying to look casual and avoiding the referee's glares. It took all the fun out of the break.

I had started out on the 42km run well in advance of my carefully constructed race plan and ahead of other competitors in my 60–65-year age group. But I didn't feel good. 'Surely this must pass,'

I thought. You tend to go through rough patches during endurance events, and easing off a fraction and taking in some energy can get you back on track.

Not this time. I felt steadily worse and my run reduced to a shuffle. The heat was unbearable. At every aid station I put ice in my tri-suit and under my cap and drank as much as I could. But it didn't work, and I was passed by a steady stream of athletes, including some from my age group. My world narrowed to the bit of asphalt just in front of my feet. Aid stations with drinks, ice and food were one mile apart. They became my target.

I'd worked out why so many ironman athletes wore shades and sunhats. It's not to be protected from the sun, nor to look cool; the sole purpose is to have something to hide behind when the going gets tough. My three-year-old grandson does it. He covers his eyes with his hands in the belief that it makes him invisible to the outside world. It worked for me; I hid my misery from the world behind my cap and sunglasses. It was just me and the asphalt and no one else.

I'd promised myself not to walk during the marathon. John Newsom – whom I coached for many years, and who is now a well-known triathlon coach himself – had chuckled when I confessed to him I was going to do the Hawaii Ironman. 'Watch out for the death march,' he warned, implying that along with the majority of the field I would succumb to the inevitable walk during the final 10km of the race. But I was determined my victory was going to be in not walking.

>>>

Now, with only 4km to go, I'm not running or even walking but at a standstill, legs apart, bent over, and hands on my thighs to support my upper body, which is swaying from side to side.

Palani Hill also goes by the name of Heartbreak Hill. It was there in 1989 that Mark 'The Grip' Allen finally broke the back of his mission to finally depose the undisputed King of Kona, Dave 'The Man' Scott. They battled side-by-side for eight hours, well ahead of the rest of the field, neither giving an inch. Halfway up Heartbreak Hill, Mark made a decisive move to break the curse that had bedevilled him in previous years when trying to wrest the race from Dave.

Here I am, right at the point where Mark made history, and I'm crumbling. I hear a faint sound of music in the distance. I think I must be hallucinating. I manage a hoarse laugh. I might as well go out with a fanfare. It takes all my energy to lift my head to look up the road to the top of the hill.

Through the haze created by the heat I can see people dancing. 'Shit, is that for real?' I start to urge myself on. 'C'mon, John, get to the music.' I quicken my pace, but I'm still not running. I feel drawn to the music as if by a magnet. There's a group of young people … I register bare chests, tee-shirts wrapped around heads, long dreadlocks, happy faces, beer bottles swinging from their hands … some of them break away from the group and come towards me, dancing, singing and yelling.

'What are they saying? Who are they?' They form a circle around me and now I can hear them: 'C'mon, old man, you can do it, use the beat of the music.' I repeat: 'C'mon, use the beat of the music.' And again: 'Use the beat of the music.' My legs get the message and start to move as if I have no control over them. Hesitant at first, they try to follow the beat.

The young people dance next to me to the top of the hill. 'Come with me,' I want to shout, but nothing comes out. All my energy goes into absorbing the rhythm of the music and transforming it into forward momentum. From the top of the hill it's all downhill to the finish. 'I can make it, as long as I stay upright and put one foot in front of the other.' I concentrate on doing just that.

I'm greeted just before the finish line by the relieved faces of my support crew, consisting of Ien, my niece Jasmijn and her partner, Rubert. I hear the legendary voice of Mike Reilly call out over the microphone: 'Number 289, John Heeeelleeeemaaaans. You are an Ironman.' Am I ever.

Reality check

It took a long time to recover from the Hawaii Ironman and I did not compete in any events for more than a year. In the winter of 2015 I ran in the 8km-long Holloway Memorial Cross Country Race, an event on the regional running calendar with a long tradition and rich history. It was staged at the grounds where the QE2 Sports Stadium once stood, a place where I spent a significant part of my New Zealand life working and playing (read training). This once-famous sports complex, built for the 1974 Commonwealth Games, was one of the many victims of the 2011 Christchurch earthquake. It felt weird and somehow wrong to be there now, looking at green spaces and ruins where this landmark had been.

But there was business to attend to. About 800m into the race, I felt good, and ready to put my foot down and work myself up the order. Then something unusual happened. A tight band formed around my chest and I had difficulty breathing. This had never happened to me before. 'Blown a gasket,' was my first thought. Then: 'Don't be a wimp.' I tried to up the pace despite the discomfort, but the body didn't respond. Instead, I nearly passed out. I backed off to a slow jog. Usually, that's enough to get out of a bad patch. The pain eased a fraction, but the legs stayed heavy and the breathing laboured. This was ridiculous. I thought about pulling out, but knew I couldn't.

Rightly, my family had long since become bored with my sporting escapades and didn't come to watch and cheer any more. I couldn't blame them. It's not a pretty sight, the geriatric brigade struggling around a course in different stages of distress. At that age there's still plenty of ambition, but not the energy nor the physique to fulfil it. At this particular event on this particular day, as fate would have it, who should have turned up to cheer me on but Ien and our two granddaughters, six-year-old Ocean and Lakey, aged three. 'C'mon, Opa,' I heard them yell from a distance. When I jogged past, Lakey was hesitantly waving her little hand at the runner just ahead of me; to her, we must have looked all the same, a bunch of cotton-tops in our running gear.

Ocean joined me and ran alongside me with ease. Before her school cross country race a few weeks earlier, I had given her a bit of a lecture to the effect that you should never give up in sport; you have to keep going and stick it out. That put me in a dilemma. There was no way I could quit now, and so I struggled on, slowly drifting back to the rear end of the field. Ocean accompanied me over the finishing line. I felt wretched.

Ocean observed that I was soaking wet and asked if I'd had to run through water. I was sweating excessively, considering the air temperature was barely above 10°C. 'No darling, that's called sweat. Your skin produces it when you work really hard.' She took a final curious glance at my dripping face before losing interest and dancing away.

I felt my pulse. It was fast and irregular. Perhaps it would settle by itself. We took the grandkids to the beach down the road, dug a big hole and messed about under a subdued autumn sky. But all was not well. On returning home, I found things had not improved, so I rang a colleague for advice. 'Straight to the emergency department,' he said sternly, and I knew he was right.

Within no time, I was hooked up to a daunting array of drips and monitors that emitted an unsettling cacophony of buzzes, bells, beeps and whizzes, like an electric orchestra tuning up.

I'd had suffered from exercise-induced atrial fibrillation, a rhythm disturbance of my heart, not uncommon in endurance athletes. With the realisation sinking in that this was probably going to spell the end of my competitive career, I was whisked away to the ward, tethered to the lifesaving technology that had started to look life-threatening to me. I took a sleeping pill and closed my eyes. I felt like an old man – there was no denying it now – as I looked back over my hectic life. Everyone would say I'd had a good innings as a competitor. Had it all been worth it? I wasn't bitter, a little cynical perhaps. I'd always tried to live up to my ideal of never giving up, and as an athlete that had meant staying upright to the bitter end, no matter what the physical cost. I'd always got away with it before but here I was now, flat on my back, wondering whether I'd pushed it too far this time. I had a lot to live for – Ien, my daughters, the wonder of grandchildren; even if this was the end of competing for me, classical music and good books would provide solace – and I wasn't ready to give up any of that. I drifted off into an uneasy sleep.

Epilogue

Following my cardiac event I took a year off from competition. I did force myself to exercise for my health, as you can't just suddenly stop when you've trained all your life.

It felt like an obligation rather than fun. I slowly got my mojo back, and in April 2016 took part in the Sea2Sky event, the first triathlon staged in Christchurch since the earthquake, held around Sumner and my favourite terrain, the Port Hills. I was just happy to be there, but the 'top end' was missing.

Early in 2017, I made the mistake of doing the Wanaka Challenge 70.3 event (2km swim, 90km bike and 21km run). 'I'll just take it easy,' I thought. 'Surely I can complete the distance comfortably that way.' But despite 'taking it easy', I was forced to sit down on the side of the road for a while, where I thought dark thoughts. The mind had been willing but clearly the body had had enough.

I went to my old battleground along the foreshore of Auckland one more time for the World Masters Games in April the same year. I managed to squeeze a final effort out of my protesting body for a win in my age category. I made sure to leave any residual competitive desire behind at the finish line.

After my stint in Holland with the Dutch triathlon team I returned to practising sports medicine. I still coach and advise a few elite athletes, I am an advisor for the national Triathlon High Performance Programme and am part of the coaching staff for the Canterbury Triathlon Academy, a programme which provides young, regional triathletes with a pathway towards national and international success.

>>>

In 2018 I did the Tour of Aotearoa, a self-supported mountain bike ride following tracks the length of New Zealand.[1] It was not a race, so I thought it would be okay: 3000km over 30 days, 100km per day, did not sound too onerous. But being more experienced with road biking than with (heavily loaded) mountain biking I had underestimated the event. I still had plenty of ambition but it was being thwarted by multiple ailments and dwindling energy reserves, and I was missing Ien. One morning on day 12, feeling particularly grim and disheartened, I was sitting in a café for breakfast when a text message pinged its arrival. It was from my good friend Renzie Hanham.

> Renzie: How are you feeling this morning?
> Me: Not great, not sure why I am doing this.
> Renzie: I just read your last blog. I guess it will come down to the meaning and significance this has for you, not that you need me to tell you that!
> Me: Is it about not giving up?
> Renzie: It's what underpins that and what gives that meaning. Never giving up is a useful attribute … often.
> Me: Well, I better get on with it for a bit more, over and out.

Of course, Renzie's insightful questions and comments offered me a way out if I wanted one – all I had to do was decide whether finishing the Tour was really important to me. The question mark stayed with me for the rest of the event, and found its way into the title of this book.

Notes

CHAPTER 1: ERIN BAKER

1 Drafting is the act of riding close behind another cyclist to avoid frontal resistance created by the wind. The leading rider 'breaks' the wind, which creates an area of reduced air pressure in their wake. This results in energy savings of up to 30% for riders sitting in the wake. Triathlon is considered an 'individual' sport, and drafting is generally not permitted. A distance of 10m between bikes needs to be maintained unless passing. As this rule became increasingly difficult to referee in the closely-fought elite races, from 1996 the International Triathlon Union allowed drafting in events over the shorter Olympic and sprint distances. Age-group races and events over the longer ironman and half ironman distances are still 'non-drafting' events. The rule is hotly debated by officials and athletes, as it is difficult to interpret accurately from the pillion seats of motorbikes, where the referees are seated.

2 Erin Baker won 104 of the 121 races she entered. She was named New Zealand Sportswoman of the Year and Supreme Award winner at the 1989 Halberg Awards. Erin was made a Member of the Order of the British Empire (MBE) in 1993 for services as a triathlete. In 1995 she was inducted into the New Zealand Sport Hall of Fame, in 2017 into the ITU Hall of Fame and in 2018 into the Ironman Hall of Fame.

CHAPTER 2: GROWING PAINS

1 I later discovered that the phrase – variations on 'What if they gave a war and nobody came' – is from a poem by Bertold Brecht, written in the 1930s. The poem ends 'Even avoiding battle will not avoid battle / Since not to fight for your own cause / Really means / Fighting on behalf of your enemy's cause'.

2 Opa is 'grandfather' in Dutch.

3 Had it not been for a couple of colossal rowers from Romania, who won the race by more than a boat length, they would have been Olympic champions. Romania was the only Eastern Bloc country not to boycott the games that year.

CHAPTER 3: DOWN UNDER

1 The phrase is from John Lennon's remarks about his 1968 song 'Revolution': 'The statement in "Revolution" was mine. The lyrics stand today. ... Count me out if it's for violence. Don't expect me on the barricades unless it is with flowers.' *Playboy*, 1980.

2 Compulsory army service, introduced under the occupation of Napoleon in 1810, was abolished in Holland in 1997.

3 Graham Smart was awarded Member of the New Zealand Order of Merit (MNZM) for services to medicine and the community in the 2004 New Year Honours List.

4 The Takahe-to-Akaroa relay is New Zealand's oldest running relay, first held in 1935. The race starts at the Sign of the Takahe in the Port Hills of Christchurch

and finishes in Akaroa. The total distance is 76km. Sections of varying distances and terrain are divided among eight athletes in each team.

5   S&B Foods is the Japanese spices company responsible for introducing wasabi in a tube to the world in 1970.

CHAPTER 4: TRIUMPHS AND TRIBULATIONS

1   Les McDonald died on 4 September 2017 in Vancouver, at the age of 84. Less than two weeks later, on 13 September, the ITU inducted Joop van Zanten into the ITU Hall of Fame for the work he had done for the European Triathlon Union.

2   Blood doping is the practice of boosting the number of oxygen-carrying red blood cells by taking a blood transfusion with your own, previously stored, blood. The infusion takes place after the body has naturally replenished the blood. The result is an abundance of red blood cells in the circulation, increasing the ability to carry more oxygen to the working muscles to assist energy production. The practice was common in the 1980s among professional cyclists, and to a lesser extent with middle- and long-distance runners. It was banned in 1986, but it is difficult to detect and it's likely the unscrupulous still use it in more sophisticated ways. Lance Armstrong used it for many years without discovery and despite being subject to an intensive drug-testing regime.

3   Goof Schep redeemed himself later with the discovery of the cause of a baffling condition affecting competitive cyclists. The main symptom is a rapid loss of power of the big thigh muscles when racing hard. Goof found the prolonged bent-over position causes kinking of the main arteries in the groin area, thereby cutting off blood supply to the legs when the muscles need it more than ever. Over time, this kinking results in thickening of the blood vessel wall, interfering even more with blood flow and therefore oxygen supply to the working muscles. The solution is to replace the damaged piece of artery with a graft taken from a large vein elsewhere in the body. Goof has become world famous for his discovery; my discovery of 'aero-neck' never received the same acclaim.

4   In racewalking it is ruled that the back (push-off) foot must not leave the ground until the front (recovery) foot touches the ground – an extremely difficult rule to referee.

CHAPTER 5: THE COACH

1   In 2018 Scott Molina was inducted into the Ironman Hall of Fame.

2   The academy later became known as the New Zealand Triathlon High Performance Programme.

3   Ben retired soon after the Sydney Olympics, frustrated by recurring sickness and injuries. He got into coaching, first for the Hong Kong team, then a breakthrough came when he got a coaching job with British Triathlon. He was the men's coach for the London Olympics and was appointed head coach for the Olympic programme in 2013.

4   Our muscles are made up of two different cells, also called fibres, termed slow-twitch (type I) and fast-twitch (type II). Slow-twitch muscle fibres are mainly engaged in endurance activities, while fast-twitch fibres are used in powerful bursts of movements like sprinting.

5   A domestique is an athlete who works for the benefit of the team rather than trying to win the race.

6   See Christopher J. Case et al. *The Haywire Heart: How Too Much Exercise Can Kill You, and What You Can Do To Protect Your Heart*, VeloPress 2017. A landmark paper identifying the risk of arrhythmia in

endurance athletes was published in 2013: K. Andersen et al. 'Risk of Arrhythmias in 52755 Long-distance Cross-country Skiers: A Cohort Study', *European Heart Journal*, 2013, 34(47), 3624–31.

7 Ironically, considering this aspect of his preparation, the air was clearer than it had been in decades thanks to pollution controls undertaken for the Games, and during the Oympics the citizens of Beijing re-discovered the sun.

8 In Māori society, kaumātua are elders who provide leadership and preserve the tradition and knowledge of Māori customs.

9 After the Rio Olympics Andrea went on to win ITU Triathlon World Series races in Abu Dhabi and the Gold Coast in 2017, and she earned a bronze medal as a member of the New Zealand mixed team relay at the Commonwealth Games on the Gold Coast in 2018. In recognition of her services to triathlon Andrea was appointed Member of the New Zealand Order of Merit (MNZM) in the 2018 Queen's Birthday Honours.

10 A percentage of the author's royalties from the sale of this book will be donated to the AH Foundation.
For information about the AH Foundation, email: philanthropy@pgtrust.co.nz or phone: 0800 878782.

CHAPTER 6: GOING DUTCH

1 Much research in gender differences in performance motivation has been done in the workplace. In less competitive situations women work better together than men but when competition kicks in males tend to perform better as a team than females (Markus Baer et al. 'Intergroup Competition as a Double-Edged Sword: How Sex Composition Regulates the Effects of Competition on Group Creativity', *Organization Science*, 2014,

25(3), 653–967 DOI: 10.1287/orsc.2013.0878). There is less information available on this particular topic in relation to the sporting arena but there is no reason to believe that the genders react differently in team situations in competitive sports (Joan van der Horn, 'Mars en Venus op het Sportveld: Genderverschillen in Prestatiemotivatie' [my translation: 'Mars and Venus on the Sports Field: Gender Differences in Performance Motivation'], *Sportpsychologie Bulletin*, 2004, 15, 9-14.9).

2 Liquefaction is something that people in Canterbury became very familiar with, as many areas of the region were affected by this phenomenon post-quakes. It's a process where loose, sandy or wet soil responds to earthquake shaking by behaving more like a liquid than a solid; water is forced up to the surface through cracks in the ground, resulting in a thick layer of grey silt.

3 Australian Steven Bradbury won the Olympic gold medal at the 2002 Winter Olympics over the 1000m short track ice speed-skating event as a rank outsider. He reached the semi-finals through the disqualification of one of his opponents. In the semi-final, he was riding in dead last position, when three of his four opponents crashed with the finish line in sight. The same happened in the final, but this time to all his opponents. Steven was again too far behind to get caught in the melee and crossed the finish line first, while the others were still trying to untangle the mess they found themselves in. Since then 'doing a Bradbury' has become synonymous with winning against all odds.

CHAPTER 7: THE CHALLENGE OF STAYING UPRIGHT

1 https://www.travelblog.org/Oceania/New-Zealand/South-Island/Christchurch/blog-1010366.html

Acknowledgements

My mother was a prolific reader and writer. Writing letters was her favourite form of self-expression and after we'd immigrated to New Zealand we looked forward every week to her delightfully phrased letters, full of quotes and poems, written in her distinctively neat and cursive script, each one a pleasure to the eye. She had always encouraged her children to read and I can still see the delight on her face when, in my early twenties, I told her that Charles Dickens was my favourite 19th-century writer. I will forever be grateful to my mother for passing on to me her love of the written word.

In 2014, I attended a creative writing course run by Christchurch-based writer and poet Grant Hindin Miller with the intention of developing a collection of stories and personal memories for my children and grandchildren; some of those stories made their way into this book. It was a safe entrée into the world of writing and I'm thankful to Grant for giving me the tools and confidence to continue writing for a wider audience.

I received valuable editorial feedback on earlier drafts of this book from a number of trusted friends, mentors and writing experts, and I am especially grateful to Jim Tucker, Karen Zelas, Gaike Knottenbelt, Professor Gregor Coster and Maarten Elink-Schuurman.

A special thanks goes to Canterbury University Press publisher Catherine Montgomery and to copyeditor Antoinette Wilson, who were firm but patient and respectful with their feedback. In the editing process some stories did not survive; they can wait for another time.

I am grateful to the athletes and coaches who are the subjects of many of the stories I tell. They gave me valuable feedback on the content – some recalled their experience of certain incidents differently, or did not remember them at all, but they acknowledged and respected the fact that ultimately this is my book, reflecting my memories.

Erin Baker not only kick-started my coaching career, but is also the subject of what is arguably the best story in the book. On top of that, she provided the book with a generous Foreword. It was a privilege to work with her when she was an athlete and I appreciate our ongoing friendship. Thanks go to Allan McLaren, unofficial historian for the New Brighton Harriers Club, for scrutinising the parts of Chapter 3 in which I lament my exponential decline in running strength over the years. He suggested that my memory must have suffered a similar fate, as he picked up several inaccuracies.

I am grateful to Phil Briars and Rick Faulding, who filled in for me some of the missing historical facts regarding the early years of triathlon in New Zealand. Renzie Hanham offered valuable encouragement and persuaded me that writing a book was a reasonable and normal thing to do.

My family does not feature much in these pages, but that is not because they played no role in my sporting life – on the contrary, they provided me with the motivation to succeed, as I didn't want to come home empty-handed after my triathlon trips. Thanks to Fleur and Saar, my daughters, for being who they are. I hope to make up for my frequent absences and distractions during their childhood by being a good Opa to their children, my grandchildren, to whom this book is dedicated. It has not been an onerous task thus far.

Last but not least, I want to thank my wife, best friend and soulmate, Ien. For the greater part of our married life she has had to tolerate my self-indulgent sporting escapades. There were enough times when she might well have left me for someone with a more predictable work routine and a more reliable and generous income. More recently, she has had to put up with me pecking at the keyboard like an angry bird, hour after hour, writing and re-writing these stories.

Ien has been my most fervent critic and the main reason I still have my feet firmly planted on the ground, most of the time. Her pragmatic approach to life also applied to her observations on every new draft of the manuscript, which I presented to her ad nauseam. Recently she let slip that she was happy not to be married to a politician, as that would be worse than being married to a coach, or an athlete, or a doctor. I didn't ask her what it's like to be married to all three, plus a would-be author.

Index of People

Page numbers in **bold** refer to illustrations.

About the Author

Dr John Hellemans has combined his triathlon activities with a medical career since immigrating to New Zealand from Holland in 1978. John coaches at the Canterbury Triathlon Academy and advises the national High Performance Programme. He lives in Christchurch where he continues to practise sports medicine.

His previous publications include:

Erin Baker & John Hellemans, *Triathlon: The Winning Edge*, Octopus Publishing 1988

Dr J. Hellemans, *Triathlon: A Complete Guide for Training and Racing*, Reed Publishing 1993

Dr J. Hellemans, *The Training Intensity Handbook for Endurance Sport*, KinEli Publishing 2000

Dr J. Hellemans, *The Misery of Staying Upright*, Active Health 2002

Dr J. Hellemans, *The Triathlon Coach*, Active Health 2006